British Parliamentary Debates
on the
Armenian Genocide
1915–1918

Eric Avebury (foreword)
Ara Sarafian (comp., ed. and intro.)

Gomidas Institute
Princeton and London

Published by Taderon Press, PO Box 2735, Reading RG4 8GF, England by
arrangement with the Gomidas Institute

ISBN 1-903656-11-7

For comments and inquiries please contact:

Gomidas Institute	Gomidas Institute
PO Box 208	PO Box 32665
Princeton, New Jersey 08542	London W14 0XT
USA	UK

Email: *books@gomidas.org*
Web: *www.gomidas.org*

Table of Contents

Foreword by Eric Avebury   v

Introduction by Ara Sarafian   ix

Debates:

28 July 1915, Reported Massacres in Armenia *(Viscount Bryce,*
Earl of Cromer, Archbishop of Canterbury, Marquess of Crewe)   1

6 October 1915, The Armenian Massacres *(Earl of Cromer,*
Marquess of Crewe, Viscount Bryce)   5

12 October 1915, Turkey (Massacre of Armenians)
(Aneurin Williams to Sir E. Grey, Secretary of State for Foreign Affairs) 13

21 October 1915, Armenia (Massacres) *(Commander Bellairs,*
Lord Robert Cecil, Under-Secretary of State for Foreign Affairs)   14

16 November 1915, Armenian Atrocities *(Aneurin Williams,*
T. P. O'Connor, Lord Robert Cecil, Under-Secretary of State for
Foreign Affairs, Major Lane Fox)   14

23 August 1916, Armenia *(Mr. Bird, Lord Robert Cecil)*   28

21 December 1916, Armenian Massacres *(Aneurin Williams,*
Lord Robert Cecil, T. P. O'Connor)   28

1916, Massacre of Armenians *(Sir Edwin Cornwall,*
Lord Robert Cecil)   29

1917, War Situation: Prime Minister's Review...
(David Lloyd George, Prime Minister)   29

12 November 1918, Armenia *(Sir Ramsay MacDonald,*
Mr. Balfour, Secretary of State for Foreign Affairs)   30

18 November 1918, Consolidated Fund (Appropriation) Bill
(Aneurin Williams, Sir George Greenwood, Major Peel, Sir J. Spear,
Mr. Hugh Law, Mr. Ponsonby, Lord Robert Cecil Under-Secretary
of State for Foreign Affairs, Colonel Wedgewood)   31

Appendix

I. Allied Declaration of 23 May 1915(British text)   59
II. Report by the Committee on Armenian Atrocities (4 October 1915)   61
III. Two Eye-Witness Accounts of the Armenian Genocide   91

Foreword

This book is a compilation of references to the Armenian Genocide in both Houses of Parliament during and immediately after the Great War of 1914-18, together with some of the materials on which Members based their assessments. It shows that Parliament was active then, not only in drawing attention to the Genocide, but in correctly identifying it as 'absolutely premeditated and systematic'. Today, there is a great deal of additional evidence in the public domain, from the archives of the central powers and the Ottomans, and from hundreds of poignant letters and diaries of survivors and independent witnesses, confirming that initial verdict.

The debates assumed that the survivors of the Genocide would be restored to their lands under international protection, with the United States mentioned as the likely trustee power. Not to allow the Armenians to govern themselves in the areas where they were the major element before the war would 'put a premium on massacre', as Aneurin Williams said. Tragically, the commitment evaporated, just as the promises made to refugees ethnically cleansed in Bosnia have been forgotten even sooner in our own time.

Another note would be familiar to a modern audience: the Genocide was part of a policy which, according to Viscount Bryce, had been entertained for some time, but the Ottoman authorities 'hesitated to put it into practice until they thought the favourable moment had come'. As with Hitler's attempts to exterminate the Jews, there had been earlier massacres and lesser violations of human rights, but the final solution had to await the cover of a world war.

Nor could anybody reading the evidence escape the conclusion that there is another parallel with the Holocaust. As Goldhagen writes in *Hitler's Willing Executioners,* ordinary Germans were persuaded to participate actively in the murder, torture and rape of Jews because they had been thoroughly indoctrinated with the notion that Jews were evil and a threat to the German state. The Nazis added the gas chambers, but they still had the death marches, in which Jewish victims were deprived of basic human needs, given no medical attention, and shot in batches along the route. In Armenia, the death marches were the main instrument of genocide, and the accounts of survivors are uncannily similar to those of German death march survivors. And just as the ordinary Germans of the police battalions were happy to inflict unimaginable sufferings on helpless Jews without being given specific orders as to the extent and nature of the cruelties they were to perpetrate, so the Turkish guards deliberately caused the maximum torment and distress to their Armenian victims.

Without the benefit of foresight, Parliamentarians were not to know that Hitler would use the Armenian Genocide as a model, nor was the term 'genocide' yet coined at that time. Curiously enough, although repeated reference was made to 'crimes', 'massacres', 'extermination', and 'atrocities', none of the speakers suggested that the Ottoman leaders should be prosecuted, let alone that an international tribunal should be established for the purpose. Although after the war some trials were conducted under Turkish law and convictions secured against a number of the chief genocidalists, most of them escaped justice when the Kemalist revolution made headway after 1919.

There was a call for military intervention to protect the Armenians, to which Lord Robert Cecil replied on behalf of the Foreign Office that under the terms of the Armistice, the Allies had the right to occupy strategic points wherever a strategic situation arose that threatened the security of the alliance. The Government felt the demands of humanity, he said, and they would 'rightly expose themselves to the indignation of the country if they allowed further atrocities to take place in Armenia when they had the power to prevent them by military means'. Yet the British abandoned Cilicia in November 1919, while in the east, there were no Allied troops available to oppose the attack by the racist General Karabekir on Armenia in September 1920. The Allies were too busy opposing the Bolsheviks elsewhere, and Cecil had defended intervention in Russia, not on humanitarian grounds *à la* Kosovo, but on the basis of their 'offence against humanity' including the murder of one British officer in Petrograd. At that stage we could perhaps have rescued the first Armenian Republic (1918-1920) from the joint Turkish-Soviet attack which finally drove Armenia into the arms of the Soviets, and moved the Turkish-Armenian frontier eastwards.

One of the lessons to be learned from Parliament's treatment of the Armenian Genocide is the importance of good communications between Parliamentarians and the Foreign Office. After 1916, the main source of information for MPs and peers was the Blue Book, *The Treatment of Armenians in the Ottoman Empire 1915-16*, a project initiated by Viscount Bryce but commissioned by the Government from the distinguished historian Arnold Toynbee. This has been dismissed as wartime propaganda by Turkish commentators ever since, but the testimony of hundreds of witnesses cannot be so lightly dismissed. Undoubtedly it suited the British to portray the Ottoman regime in the worst possible light, but they were never accused of doctoring the evidence, which has since been abundantly corroborated by further testimonies which demonstrate that the techniques of the Genocide were reported to be the same everywhere.

The denialists seek to prevent comparisons between the Armenian Genocide and the Holocaust, which might help to distinguish the aetiology of genocide and thus to take better preventive measures against future genocides. As Robert Melsom has pointed out:

> * Both the Committee for Union and Progress and Nazis were revolutionary vanguards that were motivated by ideologies of revolutionary transformation.

> * Both movements came to power during a revolutionary interregnum after the fall of an old regime. Both Armenians and Jews were ethno-religious communities that had occupied a low or pariah status in traditional society, and both had experienced rapid progress and social mobilisation in the modern world.

> * Both genocides took place during revolutions and wars.

Parliament actively focused on the Armenian Genocide at the time, as this work shows; it has often analysed the Holocaust, and it has dealt with the attempted genocides of Bosnia and Kosovo. It has looked at the examinations by the UN of its own failures over Srebrenica and Rwanda. Perhaps now is the time to put all this experience together, and consider how Parliament and the Government could together look at the dreadful catalogue of genocides, and our joint failure to prevent them, and then to see what measures the international community might take to reinforce our defences against this greatest of all evils.

Eric Avebury
House of Lords, London
September 2002

Introduction

The First World War witnessed the first genocide of the modern era. Utilising the Ottoman state bureaucracy, telegraphic communications, and overwhelming force, the rulers of Ottoman Turkey carried out the systematic destruction of Armenians in the Ottoman Empire. While the British Government had a longstanding interest in Armenians, its understanding of the mass murder of Armenians was curtailed by Turkish and German censorship and misinformation campaigns.[*] However, as information filtered out of the Ottoman Empire, there was a delayed understanding of events by the outside world. Furthermore, any British discussion of the Armenian issue had to be sensitive not to alienate Muslims, as the Ottoman Empire was still regarded as the seat of the Caliphate by many British Muslims. This consideration was particularly important as the Ottoman Turks attempted to play the "Muslim card" with a formal declaration of *Jihad* (Holy War) against their enemies. This included sending emissaries to Muslim countries such as Iran and Afghanistan.

Despite these circumstances, information about "Armenian atrocities" were discussed in Parliament. This was mainly due to the efforts of distinguished

---

[*] British official involvement with Armenians developed after the Congress of Berlin (1878). Great Britain, as a signatory to that treaty, guaranteed the introduction of reforms in the Ottoman Empire for the safety of Armenians. The failure of such reforms, as well as two major anti-Armenian massacres in 1895-96 and 1909, heightened British interest in Armenians.

As information about the genocide of Armenian leaked to the outside world in 1915, the Turkish and German governments began denying facts in diplomatic and journalistic circles. As more information about the genocide came to the fore, these authorities began justifying the extra-ordinary measures against Armenians as matters of necessity. Their position was finally standardised in an Ottoman government White Paper which vilified Armenians as a rebellious community. For a frank insider's view of the German involvement with the Ottoman Turks and the Armenian Genocide, see the memoirs of Harry Stuermer, who was the correspondent of *Kölnische Zeitung* in Constantinople between 1915-16. Harry Stuermer, *Two War Years in Constantinople,* (London: Sterndale Classics, 2002).

Members of Parliament who were informed of events by their contacts in the Russian Empire, Switzerland, and the United States, as well as the British Foreign Office in London. Such voices were led by James Bryce, who was a former member of the British Cabinet, ambassador to the United States, a law professor at Oxford University, and a humanitarian activist. He had visited Armenia forty years earlier and authored *Transcaucasus and Ararat,* first published in 1877. Another advocate was Aneurin Williams, a longstanding liberal M.P. who was active on several Parliamentary Committees dealing with the Near East. He had become the Chairman of the British Armenia Committee in 1912. Other supporters included Noel Buxton, former chairman of the Parliamentary Balkan Committee and co-author of *Travels and Politics in Armenia,* and the Irish nationalist Member of Parliament, T. P. O'Connor.

Starting with qualified discussions in July 1915, the Armenian Genocide was first introduced for serious discussion by James Bryce at the House of Lords (October 6th, 1915), and then by Aneurin Williams at the House of Commons (November 16th, 1915). The definitive statement of an official thesis was the 1916 British Parliamentary report, *The Treatment of Armenians in the Ottoman Empire, 1915–16.*[*] The turning point in these developments came with the mounting evidence, especially following the release of official United States documents in October 1915 (See Appendix II). Such materials undercut the censorship and misinformation campaigns against Armenians and paved the way for the official British thesis on the Armenian Genocide.

Today the British articulation of the Armenian Genocide thesis represents a specific episode in British Parliamentary history between 1915 and 1918. These discussions were remarkably grounded, with participants taking care not to overstate the case against the Ottoman Turks and their German allies. Once the reality of the Genocide became evident, the subject was integrated into wider debates on the eventual settlement of the Great War. The whole Armenian matter, however, was abandoned in the aftermath of WWI, with the ascendancy

---

[*] For a critical edition of the 1916 publication see Ara Sarafian (ed.), *The Treatment of Armenians in the Ottoman Empire, 1915-16: Documents presented to Viscount Grey of Fallodon by Viscount Bryce [Uncensored Edition],* Princeton: Gomidas Institute Books, 2000.

of the Kemalist Turks, complications brought about by the Bolshevik Revolution, and imperial rivalries amongst the remaining Allied Powers.

The present publication demonstrates the intellectual trajectory of British understanding of the Armenian Genocide in Parliamentary discussions between 1915 and 1918. These discussions were framed in formal debates, incidental references during other debates, as well as responses to oral and written questions in the Houses of Parliament. In reproducing these exchanges, we have annotated them with references to the private papers of James Bryce, the main exponent for Armenians, as well as the papers of Lord Cromer, the Under-Secretary of State, and extant foreign office materials at the Public Record Office. The supplemental materials at the end of the work show: The British version of the Allied declaration of May 23rd 1915 regarding the culpability of Ottoman leaders for the treatment of Armenians; the October 4th 1915 press release by the Committee on Armenian Atrocities in New York, probably the singlemost important document which informed the British government of the Armenian Genocide; other prime examples of documentary evidence on the Armenian Genocide in British hands. Such reports were circulated in official British circles, though they were not always published.

* * *

The present publication supplements the 1916 Parliamentary Blue Book, *The Treatment of Armenians in the Ottoman Empire, 1915-16,* which was the definitive British thesis on the Armenian Genocide. I would like to thank Eric Avebury who first suggested this project, as well as friends of the Gomidas Institute who helped with the work.

Ara Sarafian,
Gomidas Institute (UK), London,
August 2002

British Parliamentary Debates
on the
Armenian Genocide
1915–1918

REPORTED MASSACRES IN ARMENIA.[*]

VISCOUNT BRYCE had the following Question on the Paper—

To ask the Lord President of the Council whether His Majesty's Government have any information regarding the massacres of the Christian inhabitants which are reported to have been committed by the Turks in the districts of Zeitun, Mush, Diarbekir, Bitlis, and elsewhere in the region inhabited by the Armenians; and regarding a reported wholesale deportation of the inhabitants of some districts into Central Asia Minor and the desert parts of Mesopotamia; and whether, if these reports are well-founded, there is in the opinion of the Government any step that can be taken to save what remains of the Christian population of Armenia.

The noble Viscount said: My Lords, I cannot say, how far it is likely that His Majesty's Government will have any considerable amount of definite and accurate information upon which they can rely regarding what is supposed to have been done in Eastern Asia Minor, Armenia, and elsewhere; but from what information has reached me I have little doubt that terrible massacres have been committed. This information comes partly from Tiflis, partly from Petrograd, and partly from Constantinople to Switzerland and Paris. The stories are that all through Armenia in the Taurus Mountains and north-eastwards towards the Russian and Persian frontiers, and particularly in the districts of Zeitun, Mush, Diarbekir, and Bitlis, there have been extensive massacres in which large numbers of Christians have perished. I hope my information may be exaggerated, as reports in the East often are, and if there is any information in the possession of His Majesty's Government which can mitigate the account of the horrors we shall be only too glad to have it.

According to my information there was, at Mush in particular, a very extensive massacre; at another place all the male population that could be seized were brought out and shot, and women and children to the number of 9,000 were taken to the banks of the Tigris and thrown into the river and drowned. Similar horrors are reported from other places, particularly at Zeitun, where the inhabitants are a warlike race. These people occupied a valley which was difficult of access; they were summoned by the Turks to serve in the Army, and when they threatened to resist, the Turks prepared an expedition to attack Zeitun and proceeded to enter the passes. The passes were well guarded

---

[*] House of Lords, *Hansard* (5th series), Vol. XIX, 28 July 1915, col. 774-78. The Foreign Office minutes at the Public Record Office provide the following background to Bryce's question: "I have discussed this with Lord Bryce. He does not expect any elaborate declaration of policy and is only putting the question with a view to advertise the situation and give HMG an opportunity of advertising it. He thought HMG might be prepared to say that these facts would not be forgotten in deciding the fate of Turkish rule after the war, but quite realises that such a statement might be inopportune." See FO371/2488/108070

and the people were able to defend themselves tolerably well. But a message was sent up from the Turkish Governor of some of the towns lower down in the plain warning the people of Zeitun that if they offered further resistance the Armenian population of those towns would be wiped out. Under this threat the Zeitunlis consented to admit the Turks into the upper part of the valley where the town lies. When the Turks got there they immediately seized the inhabitants, carrying off the women and children and such of the men who did not succeed in escaping to the mountains. And so far from keeping their promise the Turks did not spare the inhabitants of the villages below. From the accounts that have reached me I understand that in some cases the whole population has been practically deported, sent off some of them into Central Asia Minor, particularly to the neighbourhood of Angora, where they were placed in a marshy and unhealthy spot. Some of them were sent to the Desert of Zor in Mesopotamia, where they experience great difficulty in supplying themselves with food, and where they are exposed to neighbouring nomadic Arab tribes.

As far as I know, these are the facts of the case. It would appear that the whole purpose of Sultan Abdul Hamid to do what he could to exterminate the Christian population is now being carried out with frightful effectiveness, and in some places I understand that Moslems from other parts of the country are being brought in to fill the void which has been left by the

extermination of the Christians. Of course, the Kurds have played a leading part; and those of your Lordships who remember the terrible events of 1895 and 1896 will recall what the Kurds were then guilty of, and it is needless to say that their present participation has been accompanied by numerous outrages upon women. I do not know whether it is possible under existing circumstances that much, if anything, can be done. Still I think it is right that your Lordships should know these facts, and if His Majesty's Government can give us any information we shall be glad to have it.

Some three months ago, when the Turkish authorities in European Turkey were threatening to put to death the Armenians in large numbers—they have in point of fact executed a good number of persons upon charges of "conspiracy"—a warning was given by our Foreign Office, possibly by the Allied Powers generally, that those responsible for such crimes would be held guilty at the end of the war and that there would be an endeavour to see that condign punishment should be inflicted upon them. I do not know whether there is any way of bringing to the knowledge of the Turkish Government—perhaps it could be done through the American Embassy—that their conduct now could not fail to be remembered and would affect whatever action the Allied Powers might take at the conclusion of the war. Whether any good would be done by a step of that kind I must leave it to His Majesty's Government to determine. But in any case I hope they will bear the matter in mind, and will draw further the conclusion that the faults of the Turkish Government are incurable, and that we cannot hope that anything less than the most drastic measures will be sufficient, when the time comes for us to consider remedial measures, to secure the safety of the unfortunate Christian inhabitants in that country.

THE EARL OF CROMER: My Lords, I fully sympathise, and I am certain that His Majesty's Government will, with the spirit which has inspired the noble Viscount in putting his Question. As we all know, the lot of the Armenians in the past has been terrible, and we also know the persistent interest which the noble Viscount has taken in their lot for a long while. I am afraid that their hardships have not been mitigated by the rising German influence in Turkey; I should think rather the contrary. The difficulty is to know what to do, and I confess I have no more practical suggestions to make than those which the noble Viscount has made. The only thing to do would be, through the American Ambassador, to call the renewed notice of the Ottoman Government to the matter. At any rate, it would have the effect of again drawing the attention of that Government to the position of these unfortunate people, and perhaps alleviate their lot a little. More than that I am afraid we cannot do.

THE LORD ARCHBISHOP OF CANTERBURY: My Lords, I think the House and the country should be grateful to the noble Viscount for bringing this question to public notice—public notice, it may be, abroad as well as at home. It falls to me, in circumstances with which I need not trouble your Lordships, to be in frequent communication with those who have had to do with Christians in a somewhat different region though not far remote from that to which the noble Viscount referred—Christians on the Turkish and Persian borders where the Kurds abound, in Urumiah. I have had letters during the last few months giving appalling accounts of the wrongs and massacres that have been perpetrated by the Turks during their temporary occupation of territory now occupied by the Russians. Among the most pitiable parts of the communications was the wail put up by those who wrote that nobody in Europe seemed to know or care anything about the matter. I cannot help feeling that such words as have been spoken by the noble Viscount and the noble Earl to-night will show those whom they may ultimately reach, and their friends elsewhere, that it is not at all events without a desire to show such sympathy as may be practicable that we hear accounts of the horrors that have taken place. At this moment the Russians occupy Urumiah, and the plain country at the bottom of the mountains is also in the hands of the Russians; and it is not unimportant that it should be known by our Ally that we have feelings of intense horror at what has happened in these districts during their occupation by the Turks. Ineffective as anything that may be said here to-night may be, it should not be entirely useless, for it will show that we are endeavouring to extend as much influence as we can to bring about an amelioration of the lot of those people, the horror of which it is almost impossible to exaggerate. If the noble Viscount has been correctly informed as to the condition of things then it is approaching the extermination of the Christian population in this region which we hope is to be in future dominated under Christian auspices. It is well that it should be known that our eyes are not entirely blind to the horrors which require alleviation and to the wrongs we desire to see punished.

THE MARQUESS OF CREWE: My Lords, I am grieved to say that the information in the possession of the Foreign Office on the subject which my noble friend has raised, although it is not much more ample than that of which he is possessed, is in conformity with what he has told us. I fear that there can be no doubt that the general facts are as my noble friend has described them. The noble Viscount and the most rev. Primate have reminded the House that some two months ago, in concert with the Governments of France and Russia, representations were made in regard to the massacres which had been perpetrated up to that date, May 24, to the effect that members of the Ottoman Government and all their agents who could be shown to be actually implicated would be held personally responsible for the crimes that had taken place. Since then the crimes have increased in number, and, if possible, in atrocity. Wholesale massacre and wholesale deportation have been carried out under the guise of enforced evacuation of particular villages, and there have been a series of other outrages such as my noble friend has described. In addition there have been the particular cases, of which the most rev. Primate alluded, of similar crimes committed against the Nestorian Christians on the Persian border. It is also we believe true, as the noble Earl opposite indicated, that these crimes have been countenanced, if not in some cases actually encouraged, by the German officials in Turkey, whose presence there and the influence which they have exercised has been an absolute and unmitigated curse both to the Christian and Moslem populations of Turkey. These officials have shown a most cynical disregard of the welfare of the country and of all the people who inhabit it. It is true, as has been stated by all the speakers, that for reasons quite obvious to anybody who follows the progress of the war there are no immediate steps which we can take for the actual repression of these atrocities. All that we can do at the moment is to repeat, and repeat with emphasis, the expression of our determination, rendered more emphatic as the weeks go on and bring fresh evidence of these crimes, that those who can be held to be responsible for them, whether by their direct commission or by their inspiration—and all the more I am tempted to say the higher and the more responsible the positions they hold— should receive punishment accordingly.

[House adjourned at ten minutes before Seven o'clock, till Tomorrow, Three o'clock.]

THE ARMENIAN MASSACRES.[*]
THE EARL OF CROMER rose to ask—

(1) Whether His Majesty's Government have received any information confirmatory of the statements made in the Press to the effect that renewed massacres of Armenians have taken place on a large scale;

(2) Whether the statements made that German Consular officials have been privy to these massacres rest on any substantial evidence; and

(3) Whether any further communications have recently

---

[*] House of Lords, *Hansard* (5th series) Vol. XIX, 6 October 1915, cols. 994-1004. In a private letter to Lord Crewe (dated Oct. 2, 1915), Lord Cromer explained the reasons for asking his Parliamentary question: "I send you a copy of a question which I have put down to ask in the House of Lords next Wednesday. I need hardly say that if it would cause the least embarrassment I will withdraw it, but I hardly think that this is likely to be the case. I may mention that my principal reason for asking it is that I think it very desirable at present to give the utmost publicity to the Turkish proceedings, with a view to letting the educated Mahommedans in India know what is the nature of the Turkish government, and so bring home to their minds that it would be a great mistake in any way to identify the cause of Islam with that of Turkey. I think you will agree." FO371/4288/143621

been addressed to the Porte in connection with this subject.

The noble Earl said: My Lords, the Questions down in my name, of which there are three, require but very few words of explanation. During the last few days the country has been shocked by renewed accounts of Armenian massacres which appear to have begun again on even a greater scale than those which horrified the whole civilised world a few years ago. In one newspaper I read that the number of victims amounted to as many as 800,000. The figure appears incredible, and, I should hope, is very much exaggerated. What I want to ask His Majesty's Government is whether they have any reliable information and can tell us what has actually occurred.

Again, it has been stated in the public Press that some of the German Consular officials have been privy to these atrocities to the extent even of organising and encouraging massacres. It seems almost incredible that any Government calling itself civilised, or its agents, could be party to such proceedings. On the other hand, we know from the Report of the noble Viscount, Lord Bryce, whom I am glad to see in his place this afternoon, what was the conduct of the German Army in Belgium; and we also know, from the scathing indictment which has been levelled by the French Government against the conduct of the German troops in France, what has been their conduct there. Moreover, apart from what may be the opinion of the German

Government we have some evidence of what is the opinion of distinguished Germans. Just before I came to the House, I happened to take up an evening paper, and there I saw an extract from a letter addressed by the notorious Count Reventlow—with whose name many of your Lordships must be familiar—to a German newspaper, and it is so remarkably characteristic of the German view on this subject that I will read a short portion of it. This is what Count Reventlow says:—

> "If the Turkish authorities believe it opportune to take vigorous measures against unreliable, bloodthirsty, riotous Armenian elements, it is not only right but even their duty to do so. Turkey can always be assured that the German Empire will always be of opinion that this matter only concerns Turkey."

When Count Reventlow wrote those lines and called the Armenians bloodthirsty, he had, I think, forgotten the moral pointed by the fable of the wolf and the lamb. I do not suppose that there will be any trustworthy evidence to prove the complicity of the German Government or their agents in these massacres. But when we consider the commanding influence which is now wielded by the German Government at Constantinople, any one who knows the East will be of opinion that the German Government cannot be acquitted of a vast moral responsibility unless it can be shown that knowing the practices of the

Turkish Government in this matter they took most vigorous and energetic steps to stop the proceedings.

As regards the third Question, your Lordships may remember that shortly before the recess a brief discussion on this Armenian question was initiated by the noble Viscount, Lord Bryce. The noble Marquess, the Leader of the House, in the course of a very sympathetic reply which he gave to the noble Viscount, after stating what was obviously the case, that not much could be done under present circumstances to stop these proceedings of the Turkish Government, went on to say that some communications had been made to the Ottoman authorities in the sense of warning them of their responsibility and telling them that they would at some future occasion, if a favourable moment arrives, be called to account for their conduct. And I think it was suggested in the course of the discussion—either by the noble Viscount or myself, I forget which—that perhaps it would be advisable to make some further communications to the Ottoman authorities on this subject, either through the medium of the American Embassy or some other channel. I should like to ask His Majesty's Government whether anything of this kind has been done, and, if so, with what result. I should be the last at the present juncture to wish to ask any questions about foreign affairs which would be likely to cause embarrassment to His Majesty's Government, but I feel certain that the noble Marquess the Leader of the House and his colleagues will agree with me that in this particular case the utmost publicity is highly desirable.

There are many special reasons why the facts should be made public. In the first place, it is very desirable to lose no opportunity to let the people of this country know for what we are fighting. We are fighting for a great many things and one of the objects which I hope we may attain by the end of this war is that Armenia shall no longer, as it has done in the past and as I fear it does in the present, constitute a sort of Turkish shambles. In the second place, we have to remember that we have some 70,000,000 Mahomedan fellow-subjects, who naturally have a certain amount of sympathy with their co-religionists and would be unwilling to believe ill of them unless they have positive proof. My belief is that all the educated Mahomedans of India would look with as great a horror as we do ourselves upon the proceedings of the Turkish Government.

SEVERAL NOBLE LORDS: Hear, hear.

THE EARL OF CROMER: Only they ought to have information laid before them on which to form an opinion, and when they have that information I do not doubt that they will see that it would be almost tantamount to an insult to the Mahomedan religion and to the feelings of all right-thinking Mahomedans if they in any way identified the cause of Islam with the cause of the existing Government at Constantinople. Also I think it would be very advisable to enlighten Egyptian opinion. The generation of Egyptians which suffered from Turkish rule is now dying out, and I think it would be advisable to remind the present generation of what Turkish rule means.

There is yet one further reason why I urge publicity. We have heard within the last few days that a very important Near Eastern Christian community under the auspices of a Prince of foreign extraction and of strong pro-German proclivities, is apparently about to commit what is not only a grave political error but what I also venture to say constitutes one of the blackest acts of political ingratitude that the history of the world has ever known. I do not suppose that anything we can say either inside or outside this House is likely to reach the Bulgarian public. If I am rightly informed, the greater part of the Press of that country is in German hands. At the same time I think we ought to do all in our power at all events to show the Bulgarians what measure is being meted out to another important Christian community by those with whom they are apparently about to enter into what I must characterise as a most unnatural alliance. The Bulgarians themselves suffered, in a past which is not very remote, so severely from Turkish rule that it is almost inconceivable that they should not extend some sympathy to these poor Armenians who are suffering in parts of the Ottoman dominions.

Before I sit down I wish to make one further remark. I am not, and never have been, what is generally called a Turcophobe. I recognise the manly, virile qualities of the Turkish nation, and I think in this juncture many of them are greatly to be pitied. My own belief is that if the Turks were left to themselves they would wish to live on peaceful terms with the Western Powers, and more especially with England. Unfortunately they have fallen into the hands of a narrow clique who have not the foresight to see that by entering into this war they have for ever doomed the real independence of the Ottoman Empire; for, my Lords, I am not quite sure but what that independence would not be more threatened if the Germans were victors in this contest than if, as I hope and believe will be the case, they are ultimately vanquished. But whatever there is to be said to palliate the errors which have been committed by the Turkish nation, not one word can be said in defence of the Turkish Government, either that of the present or that of the recent past. There were many people in this country who, when the late Sultan was deposed and the Young Turk Party came into power, were charitable enough to think that a great change would come over the character of what I think Carlyle called "the unspeakable Turk." There were others, who spoke with greater knowledge of Eastern affairs, who were rather sceptical on that point and thought that the change was only skin-deep. Unfortunately the latter have turned out to be the truer prophets. Let me end by saying this. It appears, as far as I can make out, that the present Turkish Government, equally with their predecessors, have made government by

massacre part of their political system. If that be so, if we cannot do anything else, at all events we may denounce their conduct to the whole of the civilised world, and we may warn all other races, whether Christian, Mahomedan, or Hindu, that by in any way associating themselves or sympathising with the Germans and the Turks they will in the eyes of posterity secure a taint and a stain which can never be removed.

THE MARQUESS OF CREWE: My Lords, as my noble friend reminded the House, it was late in July that this question of the Armenian atrocities was last mentioned by my noble friend Lord Bryce, and I am happy, in reply to the noble Earl opposite, to give such information as I can in continuance of what I then said. I entirely agree with the noble Earl that it is advantageous that so far as we are in possession of officially confirmed facts they should be made known to the world at large. There have been communications from the British Consul at Batoum, largely founded on statements which have been published in the newspapers at Tiflis, where there is, of course, every opportunity of ascertaining what the actual facts really are, and they are of the most deplorable character.

THE EARL OF CROMER: May I ask the noble Marquess the dates?

THE MARQUESS OF CREWE: That was the first week in September. The Consul described the appalling horrors which had taken place in the district of Sassoon, where the population were absolutely exterminated except so far as some few of them were able to escape.

The whole country was completely ravaged. A certain number of well-known inhabitants succeeded in escaping to the mountains, but the slaughter of those who could not so escape was universal. Then there has been a great influx of Armenian, Chaldean, and other refugees into Urumiah and the Caucasian provinces. A vast number of refugees have arrived at Etchmiadzin and at other points of the Government of Erivan. They came chiefly from Melazgert, the Achesh districts and Van. The Consul states that about 160,000 of these have passed through Igdir and Etchmiadzin. He gives a most terrible description of their condition, ravaged by disease, many of them starving. They have been dying at the rate of at least a hundred a day. Nothing can be said in too high praise of the efforts which have been made locally to cope with this hideous condition of things. The Moscow Armenian Committee, helped by a great number of young voluntary workers from Tiflis and the other towns, hastened to the district and have done every thing that they possibly could to relieve the misery of these poor people. But very large supplies of medical comforts and of medicines and also of foodstuffs, as may be well believed when one considers what the numbers of the refugees are, are needed if their condition is to be materially alleviated. Then at Elenovka and Ahti, two other Caucasian districts beyond Mount Ararat, there are about 9,000 refugees who are in no better case than the others. It is said in one report that

unless relief is forthcoming for these it is expected that some half of them will probably die. There is also a miserable account of the refugees in Urumiah. I have not got a figure of their supposed number, but I fancy they also must be very numerous. The Russian Consul there is doing what he can to get a sanitary detachment to come down and assist them.

These are terrible facts, and I should like to say that I heartily concur with what fell from the noble Earl opposite when he stated that dreadful excesses such as these are not less revolting to Moslem subjects of His Majesty in India and to enlightened Mussulman opinion everywhere than they are to ourselves. They are, of course, in no way authorised by the precepts of Islam, and they will not be condoned by the judgment of Islam. I am also in agreement with what fell from the noble Earl when he added that these stories may well go to the heart of any European people or section of people who are disposed to bind their fortunes to those of Turkey at this moment.

We have, as my noble friend anticipated, no official confirmation of the statements which have been made that the German Consular representatives in Asia have not merely looked on at but have positively encouraged these horrors. But the statement that that has been the case has been freely made by United States observers who are in a position to form an opinion, and knowing what we know elsewhere, we are bound to state that there cannot be said to be any antecedent improbability that such is the case. The noble Earl, when dealing with the last part of his Question, alluded to the statement which I made on behalf of the Government on the last occasion, that when the day of reckoning arrives the individuals who have perpetrated or taken any part in these crimes will not be forgotten. That, of course, still holds good. There is no object in repeating a statement of that kind which was made once for all, and we have not thought that any advantage would follow from an attempt to make either direct or indirect communications to the Turkish Government on the subject. They are in possession of our views, and to reiterate them would, as we think, serve no useful purpose.

VISCOUNT BRYCE: My Lords, His Majesty's Government have, of course, been unable to obtain, except from one or two quarters, official information with regard to what has been passing in Armenia and Asiatic Turkey, so your Lordships may perhaps like to hear some further information that we have been able to glean from various accounts which have come partly from missionaries and partly from various Armenian sources of information and which bear upon the question that is now engaging the House. As the noble Marquess and the noble Earl observed, the time is past when any harm can be done by publicity; and the fuller publicity that is given to the events that have happened the better it will be, because it will be the only possible

chance that exists of arresting these massacres, if they have not been completed.

I am sorry to say that such information as has reached me from many quarters goes to show that the figure of 800,000 which the noble Earl thought incredible as a possible total for those who have been destroyed since May last is, unfortunately, quite a possible number. That is because the proceedings taken have been so absolutely premeditated and systematic. The massacres are the result of a policy which, as far as can be ascertained, has been entertained for some considerable time by the gang who are now in possession of the Government of the Turkish Empire. They hesitated to put it in practice until they thought the favourable moment had come, and that moment seems to have arrived about the month of May. That was the time when these orders were issued, orders which came down in every case from Constantinople, and which the officials found themselves obliged to carry out on pain of dismissal. As was said by the noble Marquess, there is nothing in the precepts of Islam which justifies this slaughter which has been perpetrated. In some cases the Governors, being pious and humane men, refused to carry out the orders and endeavoured to give what protection they could to the unfortunate Armenians. In two cases I have heard of the Governors being immediately dismissed for refusing to obey the orders; and the massacres were carried out.

As I have said, the procedure was exceedingly systematic. The whole population of a town was cleared out, to begin with. Some of the men were thrown into prison; the rest of the men, with the women and children, were marched out of the town. When they had got some little distance they were separated, the men being taken to some place among the hills where the soldiers or the Kurds despatched them by shooting or bayonetting. The women and children and older men were sent off under convoy of the lowest kind of soldiers—many of them drawn from gaols—to their distant destination, which was sometimes one of the unhealthy districts in the centre of Asia Minor but more frequently the large desert east of Aleppo, in the direction of the Euphrates. They were driven by the soldiers day after day; many fell by the way and many died of hunger. No provisions were given them by the Turkish Government, and they were robbed of everything they possessed, and in many cases the women were stripped naked and made to travel on in that condition. Many of the women went mad and threw away their children, being unable to carry them farther. The caravan route was marked by a line of corpses, and comparatively few seem to have arrived at the destination which was stated for them. I have had circumstantial accounts which bear every internal evidence of being veracious, and I was told by a friend who lately came home from Constantinople—he belongs to a neutral country—that he had heard many accounts at Constantinople, and that what had struck him was the comparative moderation with which these atrocities were detailed by those who had first-hand knowledge of them.

To give your Lordships one instance of the systematic way in which these massacres were carried on it may suffice to refer to the case of Trebizond, a case vouched for by the Italian Consul who was present when the slaughter was carried out, his country not having then declared war against Turkey. Orders came from Constantinople that all the Armenian Christians in Trebizond were to be killed. Many of the Moslems tried to save their Christian neighbours and offered them shelter in their houses, but the Turkish authorities were implacable. Obeying the orders which they had received, they hunted out all the Christians, gathered them together, and drove them down the streets of Trebizond, past the fortress, to the edge of the sea. There they were all put on board sailing boats, carried out some distance on the Black Sea, and there thrown overboard and drowned. The whole Armenian population of from 8,000 to 10,000 were destroyed in that way in one afternoon!* After that, any other story becomes credible; and I am sorry to say that all the stories that I have received contain similar elements of horror, intensified in some cases by stories of shocking torture. But the most pitiable case is not that of those who were killed outright, but of those unfortunate women who with their children were driven out to perish in the desert—where they have no sustenance, and where they are the victims of the wild Arab tribes around them. I am afraid it can be said that nearly the whole nation has been wiped out, and I do not think there is any case in history, certainly not since the time of Tamerlane, in which any crime so hideous and upon so large a scale has been recorded.

I should like to add that what little I have heard confirms what was said by the noble Earl—that there is no reason to believe that in this case Mussulman fanaticism came into play at all. So far as I can make out, these massacres have been viewed by Moslems with horror rather than with sympathy. It would be too much to say that they had attempted to interfere, but at any rate they have never shown approval of the conduct of the Turkish Government. I ought also to add, because this is of some importance in view of the excuses which, as we understand, the German Government are ready to give for the conduct of those who are their allies, that there is no ground for the suggestion that there had been any rising on the part of the Armenians. A certain number of Armenian volunteers

have fought on the side of the Russians in the Caucasian Army, but they came, as I understand, from the Armenian population of Trans-Caucasia. It may be that some few Armenians crossed the frontier in order to fight alongside their Armenian brethren in Trans-Caucasia for Russia, but at any rate the volunteer corps which rendered such brilliant service to the Russian Army in the first part of the war was composed of Russian Armenians living in the Caucasus. There is no excuse whatever upon any political ground for the conduct of the Turkish Government. It appears to be simply carrying out the maxim once enunciated by Sultan Abdul Hamid: "The way to get rid of the Armenian question is to get rid of the Armenians"; and it has been carried out with far more thoroughness and with far more bloodthirsty completeness by the present heads of the Turkish Government than it was in the time of Abdul Hamid.

There are still, I believe, a few places in which the Armenians, driven into the mountains, are defending themselves as best as they can. About 5,000 were taken off lately by a French cruiser on the coast of Syria, and have now been conveyed to Egypt, and they tell us that in the mountains of Sassoon—to which the noble Marquess referred—and in Northern Syria, there are still a few bands, with very limited provision of arms and munitions, defending themselves as best they can against their enemies. The whole race, therefore, is not yet extinct, so far as these refugees in the mountains go and those who have

---

* The reported mass drownings at Trebizond were based on Italian newspaper accounts, but they were not subsequently substantiated. It is true that a few Armenians were drowned at Trebizond, but the bulk of the Armenian population was deported and killed elsewhere. James Bryce modified his position in subsequent publications, including A. J. Toynbee, *Armenian Atrocities: The Murder of a Nation,* London: Hodder and Stoughton, 1915.

escaped into Trans-Caucasia; and I am sure we all wish that every effort should be made that can be made to send help to the unfortunate people who remain.

I have not been able to obtain any authentic information regarding the part taken by German officials in promoting or encouraging these massacres, and therefore it would not be right to express any opinion on the subject. But I think I may venture to say that the only chance of saving the unfortunate remnants of this ancient Christian nation is to be found in the expression of the public opinion of the world, especially that of neutral nations, which may possibly exert some influence even upon the German Government and induce them to take the only step by which the massacres can be arrested—namely, to tell the Turks that they have gone too far, and that there are some things which the public opinion of the word will not tolerate.

THE EARL OF CROMER: May I suggest to the noble Marquess that it would be a very good thing if these Consular Reports were laid before Parliament or otherwise published.[*]

THE MARQUESS OF CREWE: I will inquire for my noble friend whether that can be done.

---

[*] This was in reference to the October 4th reports from the United States, and led to the 1916 blue book *The Treatment of Armenians in the Ottoman Empire*.

ORAL ANSWERS TO QUESTIONS

WAR

TURKEY (MASSACRE OF ARMENIANS).[†]

1. Mr. ANEURIN WILLIAMS asked the Secretary of State for Foreign Affairs whether he can make any statement with regard to the deportations and massacres of Armenians in Turkey; and whether he has any official information showing that some hundreds of thousand of Armenians, mostly women, children, and elderly men, have recently been done to death in pursuance of a plan of the Turkish government?

The SECRETARY of STATE for FOREIGN AFFAIRS (Sir E. Grey): All the information on this subject in the possession of His Majesty's Government was contained in a statement made by the Marquess of Crewe, in reply to a question put by the Earl of Cromer, on the 6th of October. I can only refer the hon. Member to that statement. It goes further than is the reply to a question in this House, and therefore do not propose to read it to the House. There can be but one feeling of horror and indignation about what has been done.

[†] House of Commons, *Hansard* (5th series), Vol. LXXIV, 12 October 1915, cols. 1165-1166. Aneurin Williams informed Sir Edward Grey of his intention of asking such a question in a letter dated 27 September 1915: "I should like to put down a question to you as to the latest information you have with regard to the deportation and massacre of Armenians, and will do so unless I hear from you that it would be unwise." FO371/2488/140654

ORAL ANSWERS TO QUESTIONS

WAR

ARMENIA (MASSACRES)*

1. Commander BELLAIRS asked the Secretary of State for Foreign Affairs, in view of the refusal of the German Government to express any disapproval to Turkey concerning the systematic and wholesale massacre of Christians which has taken place in Armenia, whether he can state if any action is being taken by any neutral Power to save the situation and to protect the great American and other missionary enterprises in Asiatic Turkey?

The UNDER-SECRETARY of STATE for FOREIGN AFFAIRS (Lord Robert Cecil): I do not know what steps neutral Governments may have taken in the matter. The Vatican has made earnest and repeated appeals both to the Turkish Government to stop the massacres and to the Austro-Hungarian Governments to bring pressure to bear on the Turkish Government with the same object.

ARMENIAN ATROCITIES.†

Mr. A. WILLIAMS: ... I did not rise to continue the discussion on this question which I venture to think has been pretty well thrashed out. I rose to deal with another matter in which the armed forces of this country have a great work to perform, and in which this country as a whole has a great national responsibility arising out of the history of its foreign policy. On the 6th of October of this year there was a discussion in the House of Lords which, it is no exaggeration to say, sent a wave of horror not only over this country, but over all civilised countries. The great majority of reading and thinking people realised then for the first time that the greatest massacres in history had been taking place during the last five months. In that discussion, initiated by Lord Cromer, and in which Lord Bryce, Lord Crewe, and others took a notable part, there were laid bare the facts of a horror such as the world has never seen. There have been great conquerors who have slaughtered many thousands and perhaps up to a million men, but those occurrences have been spread over a great number of years. The Turkish authorities within the little time of five months proceeded systematically to exterminate a whole race out of their dominions. They did so not in thousands or tens of thousands, but in hundreds of thousands. One estimate states that five hundred thousand persons were killed within the five months, while according to another estimate the number was as many as

---

* House of Commons, *Hansard* (5th series), Vol. LXXIV, 21 October 1915, cols. 1970.

† House of Commons, *Hansard* (5th series), Vol. LXXV, 16 November 1915, cols. 1770-1776. Aneurin Williams interjected this contribution on the Genocide into a wider debate on military conscription. We reproduce here the section of his comments related to the Armenian issue.

eight hundred thousand killed. There have been massacres of the Armenians before this last one. Ten years ago thirty thousand were massacred, and ten years before that a hundred thousand. But those massacres, which made the world shudder at the time, shrink into insignificance beside these massacres which we have been unconsciously living through in the last six or seven months. Since that Debate took place later details have come in from many sources, from German and Swiss missionaries, from escaped refugees, from Europeans in Asiatic Turkey, and from sources of all kinds, and all supporting one another in the most astonishing way, so that the facts all hang together and so that, while perhaps it is impossible to be certain of this or that detail, there is no doubt whatever of the broad lines of the occurrences. They are not general statements, but are statements from different quarters, describing what happened at particular places at particular times, with the names of the people who suffered and with the names of the people who inflicted those horrors.

Therefore it is quite certain that the broad facts of the case are established and the broad facts are these, that in the month of May or thereabouts orders were sent through the Executive authority—that is, the "gang" as Lord Bryce called them: the gang of ruffians who call themselves the Government of Turkey at the present time— systematically to nearly all the centres in Turkey where there was any considerable Armenian population. I believe I am right in saying that these orders can be traced as having been sent to some fifty places, and a uniform procedure was adopted. The Armenians of the particular centre concerned were collected together at short notice, sometimes within a few hours. In some instances where a time had been fixed the gendarmes announced before the time, the Armenians were hustled out of their beds. Sometimes a little longer, up to ten or twelve days, but I believe never more than a fortnight, was given. It was not men of military age that were taken to be interned. Not at all. The Armenians of military age were already serving Turkey as soldiers in the ranks, except those who were exempted under the laws of Turkey. At this time the men from fifteen to seventy who had not been taken as soldiers were collected together, and for the most part shot. The older men, the women and the children, were ordered to prepare to go away to a great distance. This did not take place simply in one town, but in practically every town where there was an Armenian population of any importance. It did not occur owing to the fanaticism of one particular magistrate of one particular population. It is what took place in obedience to the orders sent round from the central authorities.

These people were marched away, under the control of gendarmes to some extent, but to a large extent under the control of gaol birds—criminals who had been taken out of the gaols for the express purpose of being put in charge of these parties of Armenians. The people were allowed to take very little money with them, and very little food was given them on the journey. In some cases they were allowed to hire carts, in which either to ride themselves or to take their few belongings. In many cases these carts were turned back after a few hours or a few days of the journey had been accomplished, and the people were obliged to go on on foot. Sometimes, when they had gone a few days' journey, they were abandoned by their guards and told that they might go on by themselves. Then, when they had gone on a few miles, Kurds or other brigands fell upon them, robbed and murdered them, violated the women, took the children, and committed every kind of outrage and horror upon them. Sometimes they were not abandoned, but the gendarmes and criminal guards worked their will upon them in every form of brutality and lust. When they came to towns they sold women and girls to the harems, sold the children to Turkish families who wanted boys or girls to work on their farms and to be brought up as Mahomedans, and even sold the children to brothels. So they went on, driving them along, the people dropping by the way from hunger, women going absolutely naked in many cases, having been robbed of their clothes; babies were born by the roadside, and the mothers were told to get up and go on, until they died. At nights women were violated by thieves and ruffians who came to the encampment; and finally, when they reached the River Euphrates, the women in many cases threw themselves into the river in order that they might escape by death from man's inhumanity.

Thus perhaps one-third, or less than one-third, of those who set out came to their destinations. What were those destinations? They were humorously called by the Turkish authorities agricultural colonies. They were, as a matter of fact, places in horrible swamps, or in some cases desert places where there was no water and no possibility of cultivation, where even the miserable Arabs, who had existed there from time immemorial, often perished from hunger. There they arrived in a perishing condition, and there those who are not yet dead are probably dying rapidly. This was the fate of the Armenians in the scattered towns. I am not talking of the Armenians in Armenia. There is a very great difference. The Armenians in the scattered towns are, for the most part, artisans, merchants, shopkeepers, or professional men. They are very largely educated people, brought up in a degree of refinement, extraordinarily in advance of the Mahomedan population of the country. They felt all the more the sufferings inflicted upon them, having been accustomed to a refined, educated, and, from a material point of view, comfortable life. The Armenians in Armenia were in a different position. They were in their own country, to a very large extent they were agriculturists, and those who remain are agriculturists still, cultivating their fields and living on the produce.

Mr. DEPUTY-SPEAKER (Mr. Whitley): I must point out to the hon. Member that this subject is in order in the present Debate only in so far as it is connected with something which the hon. Member thinks the British Government could or ought to have done, and that a general description such as he is entering upon is really wide of any possibility on the part of the Government. He began by suggesting that he was going to make a proposal as to what the Government might do. That part of the subject will be relevant to-day.

Mr. T. P. O'CONNOR: May I respectfully represent to you, Sir, that these things have been done by one of the belligerents with whom we are at war; that they have been sanctioned, if not incited, by another of the enemy belligerents; that it is possible for the Government to represent these things as one of the reasons why they require this large sum of money in order to carry the War to a successful issue; and, finally, that by arousing public attention, both at home and in neutral countries, we may help the Government to take such steps as may be necessary to bring some relief to these people. For these reasons I would strongly appeal to you, if your sense of order permits you to do so, not to limit more than you possibly can the area of the discussion.

Mr. DEPUTY-SPEAKER: I was not by any means ruling the subject out of order. If Members have that impression I was certainly misunderstood. I was only saying that it must be connected with something which the Government have left undone or could have done.

Mr. A. WILLIAMS: I am most anxious to follow your ruling. If I have transgressed the rules of order, I am sure you will attribute it to my want of experience and want of skill in these matters. My point is that there are two classes of these people, and that they are in different positions. I was going to argue that for both of these classes there is something which our Government at the present time might do, and, owing to the historical responsibilities arising out of the policy of past years, ought to do. I hope I shall be in order in pursuing my subject on those lines. The Armenians, who have been subject to deportation, hardships, and the gradual wastage of death, as I have described, still, to some extent, exist as refugees in different parts of the Turkish Empire. I have to suggest that our Government should use its very best endeavours, either by the Army, the Navy, or its other resources, to rescue these people wherever it is possible. For instance, a ship of the French Fleet saw a great red cross, and on investigation discovered that there were 4,000 Armenians who had taken refuge in the mountains between Antioch and the sea. There with a few old guns they were fighting a much superior force who were attacking them with a view to extermination. That French ship was able to take off those 4,000 people and land them in Egypt, where the whole, or the great majority of them, will be saved from the fate that threatened them. Although describing in detail similar positions of other bodies of Armenians, I should like to appeal to His Majesty's Government to give us some assurance that they will, to the very best of their power, both by our ships going up and down the coast of Asiatic Turkey, and by our troops, who are now approaching the scenes of these terrible disasters—when they are getting to Bagdad—will do everything in their power to deliver such bodies of these men as are still maintaining themselves heroically against their oppressors.

I desire to call attention to other classes of Armenians who survive at the present time, and that are outside the Turkish Empire. Inside the Turkish Empire there are practically no Armenians left. That is not literally true, of course, but there are very, very few. There were probably 1,200,000 or 1,500,000 at the beginning of this War. If it is true that 500,000 or 800,000 have been killed, then the refugees that have found their way into Russia, Egypt, Bulgaria, and elsewhere probably account for nearly the whole of the remainder of the Armenian population of Turkey. Only a comparatively few thousands are left in Turkey itself. Many of these are fighting for their lives. The refugees are mainly in the Russian Caucasus. Within Armenia proper, the Turkish authorities did not pursue this policy of deportation. They pursued the much simpler policy of straightforward massacre. They sent their troops and gendarmes to attack the people in their villages and farms. Where these people

in their mountains or in groups of villages protect themselves they sent their artillery against them and destroyed them wholesale. A large number of them were able to get away under the shelter of the Russian troops. In the ebb and flow of this War Russia has advanced and retreated, and advanced again in Armenia. In the course of these movements a large number of Armenians, escaping these wholesale massacres, have got behind the Russian troops and found their way into the Caucasus. In the Russian Caucasus at the present time there are said to be 180,000 of these refugees. Thirty thousand have died there in exile since last August, and 70,000 have probably returned through the Caucasus again to those parts of Armenia which are now in Russian occupation, or have gone into those parts of Persia where there is some sort of protection by the Russians.

In regard to these people I again urge upon His Majesty's Government to consider whether through our Consuls, if possible through grants of money, and in every way in our power, they will do something to help to save these people from destruction. They are dying by hundreds every week—I might almost say by hundreds every day. We in this country are doing what we can to send relief to them. In the United States money is being collected to relieve them. Their compatriots in the Russian Caucasus are doing exemplary work in the way of relief. They are making very great sacrifices, and working very hard.

But the number is overwhelming. In this country we received, we know, about 100,000 Belgian refugees.

[An HON. MEMBER: "200,000!"]

Well, 200,000, and even for a great rich country like this that was considered to be a very great task to undertake. If you consider the comparatively small number of Armenians living in Russia, perhaps 1,500,000, and consider their limited resources, I think we may say that they have done nobly. This we may say: in relieving the refugees no distinction is made of race or religion. Even the few Mahomedan refugees who have found their way into the Russian Caucasus, escaping from the horrors of war, are being relieved in the same way as the Christian refugees. A race that can do that in the moment of its own agony gives a very handsome guarantee of nobility of character. I wish distinctly to say that I am not appealing to His Majesty's Government in this matter as a matter of race or of religion. It is not only the Armenians who have suffered in this way; not only the Armenians that will need such help as the Government can give them. The Greeks to a large extent in many districts have suffered in much the same war. The Syrian Christians have been harassed in exactly the same manner. They have fled from the terror of the Turkish troops. The other day His Majesty's Consul at Tabriz telegraphed to this country that 25,000 Syrian refugees were close to his town, and that 10,000 more were expected

immediately. Unless, he said, relief was received promptly large numbers of them must perish.

It is not only Christians. Apparently this process of exterminating all the progressive elements of the country— what is called Ottomanising the country—extends far beyond the range of the Christians. The Zionist Jews, for some reason, have been suspected of being an enlightening force, and they, too, have been in terror. My last news from over there was that the greatest religious teacher of our time, not Christian, not Jew, but a man who represents a kind of reformed Mahomedanism or a wider religion embracing Mahomedanism and other religions, Abd-ul-Baha Abbas, a man that many of us had the honour of listening to in London a few years ago, an old man who has spent his life in doing good, has been violently taken from his home on Mount Carmel to Nazareth. What has happened to him is utterly unknown, but it is extremely likely that the worst has befallen him. This is a war against all the more intelligent reforming elements within the Ottoman Empire. Not to prolong the account of these terrible events, I will ask the Noble Lord representing His Majesty's Government on this matter to tell us that everything that is in the power of the Government—the Army, the Fleet, the Consular service— will be used to help these two classes of people—those who are defending themselves for their lives within Turkish territory, and those who have sought refuge in Russia and elsewhere I say again, we must not forget that we are in the presence of the greatest massacre probably that the world has ever known. Therefore, it behoves us, I think, to make every sacrifice and put forward every effort to relieve, if possible, suffering, and to save some thousands from death that must still occur unless all our help is forthcoming.

Mr. T. P. O'CONNOR (indistinctly heard): I am going to make some demands on the Government, to all of which I am afraid they cannot accede. I am going to ask them for money. I am going to ask them for military and naval assistance, and I am going to ask them also for diplomatic assistance. I may say that I think, after the story of the Armenian massacres, so eloquently told by my hon. Friend who preceded me, everybody will agree that the large sum of money which the Government demands is necessary and well spent in this War. I will not go over the story told by my hon. Friend. No one could have told it better. One might add a tale or two, such as the ghastly episode of women, in their despair throwing their children into the river, or into the wells by the road side to be devoured by beasts, to die of hunger, or to die of exposure. The story is so ghastly that really one staggers at it, and wonders that in this twentieth century possibilities of such cruelty still exist among any people or against any people. I am especially going to appeal to the Noble Lord for some of this money which we are about to vote, for such deeds of mercy and of assistance as were done by those magnificent French vessels which rescued so many of these poor people. But the main point on which I make this appeal is that the Noble Lord and the great Department which he represents should endeavour to bring this agony, if possible, to an end, and should, so far as possible, alleviate the sufferings.

I do not appeal to the Noble Lord to make any representation to the Turkish Government. We are at war with the Turkish Government, which seems to me one of the greatest vindications and justifications of this War, and I hope that the end of the War will, among other things, be the end of this ruthless tyranny. I do not think I could honestly ask the Noble Lord to make any appeal to Germany. There is one thing very German in this whole transaction. There is one great analogy between the Germans in Belgium and the Turks in Armenia, and that is the system and policy which underlie what might be regarded by superficial observers as mere sporadic or individual blood lust. As the Noble Lord knows far better than I do, for he has had access to documents that I have not seen, this movement was simultaneous in fifty centres, and, therefore, evidently was obeying a central impetus, a central command from the heart of the Turkish Empire. I do not, as I say, ask the Noble Lord to make any representations to Germany. I do not suppose he can make any representation to a belligerent enemy during the War. As every man in this House knows, and every man in Germany knows, and, what is very important, every man in America knows, these massacres could not have taken place without the connivance, or the sanction, or, at least, the reticence of the German Government.

We know what the German Government thinks about this. Four months after these horrors began of wholesale slaughter in cold blood of thousands of men, the slow and more painful slaughter of thousands of women and girls and children, the Chancellor of the German Empire was able to announce in the German Parliament that Germany had brought about the regeneration of Turkey. Everybody knows that throughout all this district for at least a generation, or perhaps two generations, there was not a great centre of population, there was not one of the Armenian settlements which was not the subject of active, energetic, persistent propaganda by the German Consuls. Every one of these centres of slaughter was occupied by a German Consul, knowing the country, probably knowing the language, certainly knowing the Turkish authorities, certainly on good terms with them. If one of these Consuls had only lifted his finger he could have put an end to the slaughter. Nor do I ask the Noble Lord to make any appeal to German opinion. If I were freer in the somewhat necessary limits of this Debate, I could quote from the German Press what they have said about it. Perhaps the Noble Lord will allow me some indulgence in order to read just one extract from a writer in regard to whom, if ever there is a hideous atrocity, you can rely upon his

pen not to excuse or extenuate it, but to glorify it, and the name of that gentleman is Reventlow. He wrote:—

> "If the court considers it necessary that Armenian insurrection can either go on or should be crushed so as to exclude all possibility of their repetition, then there is no murder and no atrocity, but simply measures of a justifiable and a necessary kind."

I was asked last night to define German militarism, and there is the definition in the devilish spirit of such a judgment and excuse for the cowardly massacre of 800,000 human beings, not all men, but thousands of women and children. There is another point in the speech of my Hon. Friend to which I would like to refer. To tell the truth, I feel a sense of futility in discussing the question of the Armenians at all. Like most Hon. Members, I have been here for thirty-five years, and certainly a quarter of a century, or about thirty years ago from the bench opposite I heard Lord Bryce describe as horrors worse than anything that had occurred up to that time the massacre of 300,000 by Abdul Hamid, and several tens of thousands by the Committee of Progress and Reform, but here you have the massacre of 800,000 more. The point I want to dwell upon for a moment is this: So much has been written about the Armenians that many people are disposed to think of them as a subject race, like the Kurds, that inhabit Asia Minor and other regions. Anybody who reads history knows that the Armenians are one of the most ancient and cultured, and one of the proudest in the history of civilisation and Christianity. In spite of all this massacre and persecution they have been the great rock of Christianity and the breakwater against the attacks of the Kurds. You have heard the story of these women who have been sold into the harems of the Turks. A couple of young girls were sold to a Turk for 3s. 6d., and some of them sold into prostitution. Who are these women? There is not a man in this House, however high his position, who has in his family girls of greater culture, of greater sweetness, of nobler purity, or more civilised and cultured life than these women.

We have in this great struggle one mighty nation which stands in whole relief, and which by the character of its citizens and their intense spirit of humanity can deal with this question and save some of the living, and that country is the United States of America. I can encourage the Noble Lord to make representations to the Government of that great nation by the fact that these massacres elicited in America an outburst of horror and sympathy with the Armenians as great as was ever extended to any suffering or oppressed people in the history of the world. I have been in correspondence with some of the members of the Armenian Committee* that has been formed, and they say incidentally that in

Switzerland—another neutral country —there is a strong feeling that the Noble Lord can appeal for sympathy and support in trying to bring these horrors to an end. I have met many distinguished and cultured gentlemen from Switzerland, and some of whom have actually gone to Armenia to establish industries and orphanages for the remnants of that race. We have had many thrilling and moving stories of these horrors and atrocities from those who have seen these massacres. Some of the information at our disposal in regard to these massacres in Armenia have come from German sisters. I can give the Noble Lord another ground for a strong appeal in this connection. We have tried to do something in Armenia.

Many good Englishmen, mainly connected with the Society of Friends, have conferred enormous benefits in times of crisis on the people of Armenia, but the nation that has done most for Armenia is America. Anybody who travels through the Near East, Egypt, and Armenia will know that the most beneficent agencies there are the American missions. They mainly, indeed I think entirely, belong to members of Protestant communions, entirely unsectarian in spirit. I am not going to quarrel with the religious belief of any man who devotes himself to the service of suffering. Therefore, to me it makes exactly the same appeal as if it were a mission of the Roman Catholic Church. I think they had at least fifty places of instruction in knowledge, in Christianity, and in moral conduct among these Armenian people, and they

---

* This reference is to the Committee on Armenian Atrocities (CAA), which later became the Committee for Armenian and Syrian Relief (ACASR). See Appendix II.

produced marvellous results. I hope I am not wearying the House if I just read one little extract. I may say that I take this from a penny pamphlet entitled "Armenian Atrocities: the Murder of a Nation."[*] I think every Member of the House has got a copy. I implore them to read this book, and to spread this book, because it is one of the most thrilling and most eloquent appeals that has ever been written. I want, for the purpose of strengthening the hands of the Noble Lord, in making this appeal to America to bring into juxtaposition, so far as official rules permit the work of the American mission, and the work of the Turkish ruler by one little example. I am quoting from the president of an American college in Armenia, and this president, speaking about the massacres, gives a list of the students and of the professors of this college. The Noble Lord has the pamphlet before him, and it is on page 100. Will the House listen to this:–

> "Constituency: Approximately two-thirds of the girl pupils, and six-sevenths of the boys have been taken away to death, exile, or Moslem homes. Professors: Four gone, three left, as fellows."[†]

I want just to say a word about one or two of these professors. Professor B.,[‡] who served the college thirty-three years, studied at Ann Arbor, which I may inform the House is one of the greatest educational institutes of the United States. He was a professor of mathematics. I find that another professor studied at Princeton, another university of the United States. Another professor studied at Edinburgh. He was a professor of mental and moral science. He was tortured. He had three finger-nails pulled out by the roots, and he was killed in one of the massacres. I take the case of Professor G.[**] He served the college about fifteen years. He studied at Cornell and Yale, two great educational institutes of the United States, and he was professor of biology. The professors of this college, of which the president was a citizen of the United States, received their learning in the great universities of the world, and especially in the universities of the United States, and they were massacred, tortured, or persecuted. Now you have the picture in juxtaposition: the noble work of the American mission and the hideous and diabolical work of the Turkish ruler. In my opinion there is no Power to-day which can exercise so powerful an influence on the future of this ghastly and terrible question than the Government of the United States. I am not sure whether the Foreign Office of this country can, in accordance with the

---

[*] A. J. Toynbee, *Armenian Atrocities: The Murder of a Nation,* London: Hodder and Stoughton, 1915.

[†] The report quoted was written by Ernest W. Riggs in a letter to William Peet, dated Harpoot, 19 July 1915. The original letter can be found at Houghton Library, Cambridge, Mass. USA, file number ABC, 15.9.7/25d/273. This letter was also reproduced in the Parliamentary Blue Book, *The Treatment of Armenians in the Ottoman Empire.*

[‡] Prof. Nahigian

[**] Prof. Luledjian

rules of diplomacy, make a direct representation to the President of the Government of the United States, but I do know that the Noble Lord and we here to-night can confidently appeal for sympathy and support to the generous and humane people of the United States in bringing relief to this poor and oppressed people.

The UNDER-SECRETARY of STATE for FOREIGN AFFAIRS (Lord Robert Cecil): The House has listened with rapt attention to two speeches of a very high order in describing the terrible events which have recently taken place in Armenia, and, speaking from this bench, there really is very little indeed for me to add to what my hon. Friends, one on each side of the House, have already said. The story is a terrible one. The House will recollect that before this War broke out, in February of last year, the Powers had induced the Turks to accept a measure of reform which might, I think, have produced some real amelioration and some real security for these unhappy people. I will not go into the details of it, but there were to be two Inspectors-General, who were to have certain powers, which I think would have been of value; but the moment War broke out, and even before Turkey had joined our enemy, she abandoned all pretence of accepting this reform, and as soon as she thought, or, rather, as soon as the Committee of Union and Progress thought—it is unfair to say Turkey—it could safely be done, they initiated the terrible scheme of which we see the results at the present day. I think it may be said, without the least

fear of exaggeration, that no more horrible crime has been committed in the history of the world. My hon. Friend behind me recited some of the incidents. I am not going to harrow the feelings of the House—there is really no object in doing so—by adding to the details of what has unfortunately occurred. It is enough to say that no element of horror, outrage, torture, or slaughter was absent from this crime. It was not only the slaughter and destruction of this people, but it was the slaughter of them under the cruellest possible circumstances to be imagined.

There is as far as I know only one mitigation of the horror, and it is that this was in no sense a religious movement. It was not out of any fanatical outburst of Moslem feeling. It was nothing of the kind. We had every reason to believe—and I do believe—that pious Moslems in all parts of the world view with as great reprobation as even we do the horrors which have taken place in Armenia. It had nothing to do with any religious persecution or religious hatred. Feeling against Christianity did not enter into it at all. But that very circumstance, which from one point of view is something we may congratulate ourselves upon, is, in another point of view, an aggravation of what has occurred. This is a premeditative crime determined on long ago. It is part of the deliberate policy of those who Lord Bryce so rightly called "a gang of murderous ruffians that rule Constantinople at the present time." One of them has undoubtedly, on more than one occasion—I was told only this minute—boasted to a mutual friend in Constantinople that he and his friends in six months have done more than Abdul Hamid did in thirty years. It was a long-considered, deliberate policy to destroy and wipe out of existence the Armenians in Turkey. It was systematically carried out. It was ordered from above, and when, as happened on one or two occasions, the local governors were anxious to spare some of the children, or mitigate in some degree the horrors of the operation, they were sternly ordered to go on with the work, and I believe in one or, perhaps, two cases they were removed from their offices for not carrying it out with sufficient vigour.

There is one other circumstance I am bound to remind the House of. Not only was this premeditated. There was no provocation whatever. It has been suggested by that apologist for all that is wicked—Count Reventlow—that this was merely a rough suppression of insurrection and riot. There is no truth whatever in it. There was no insurrection, no riot; nothing of the kind. It has been suggested in America that agents of this country intrigued with Armenians to stir them up to rebellion against their lawful Sovereign, and that this country is responsible for the horrors that resulted. I am quite sure the House will believe me when I assure it that no kind of truth exists for any such allegation. There have been no intrigues by this country with the Armenians to stir them up to rebellion. There have been no attempts to raise them against their masters, though the

House will easily see that if any such attempt had occurred it would be far from an excuse for or even palliation of the crimes committed. But even this miserably poor excuse is absolutely without foundation. The crime was a deliberate one, not to punish insurrection but to destroy the Armenian race. That was the sole object, the sole reason for it.

Mr. Deputy-Speaker was good enough to point out that though this discussion of the terrible crimes that have been committed was in order, yet it was necessary to deal with the practical proposal that was to be made in order to mitigate or save the remnants of the Armenian people. My hon. Friends made one or two proposals. My hon. Friend (Mr. A. Williams) suggested that we might instruct the Fleet, if they saw any opportunity, to save any outlying bands of fugitives. I do not know that the British sailor would need any instruction of that kind.

Mr. A. WILLIAMS: Let them look for opportunities.

Lord ROBERT CECIL: I am quite certain, if they see an opportunity, they will be only too ready to take it. It was very rightly said that the French Fleet had had an opportunity, and had saved some 4,000 Armenians. I am quite sure, if any such opportunity falls in the way of a British commander, he will be only too glad and too ready to imitate his French colleagues. The hon. Gentleman also, asked me to say, on behalf of the Government, that we would use every resource of the Army and Navy and the Consular services to assist and save the

Armenians. I am sure my hon. Friend will not misunderstand me if I do not give a pledge of that kind quite in those terms. After all, the greatest possible protection for the Armenians is our victory in this War. To that all our main efforts must be bent. Our Army and our Navy, and all our resources must be devoted to destroying the enemy, wherever we can find him, until he accepts terms of peace which will be acceptable to the Allies. But it being well understood that we must have that object before our eyes first of all, I am quite sure if any opportunity should occur to assist the Armenians by the efforts of our Consuls or of our forces in any way practicable, I am certain the Government would feel that that is a very noble use to which the resources of this country could be put.

There is one thing I will tell the House—it is a small matter—what we have already done. It bears on one suggestion. It is that we had telegraphed to the Commander of our forces (General Nixon) in Mesopotamia, and asked him to communicate with the Arab tribes and induce them, as far as possible, to assist these unhappy fugitives wherever they can. That has already been done, and I hope it may have some result. My hon. Friend (Mr. T. P. O'Connor) made another suggestion, and that was that we should make representations to neutral Governments, and he particularly mentioned the Governments of the United States and the Swiss Republic.

Mr. T. P. O'CONNOR: I made an omission that I should like to repair, and that is that you should back up some representations which I made to the Pope, who has already intervened in the matter.

Lord ROBERT CECIL: I am glad of that interruption. It enables me to say— indeed, I should have said it in any case—that humanity is grateful to His Holiness the Pope for the steps he has already taken to try and secure the safety of the Armenians. He made the strongest possible representations, as my hon. Friend knows, and if they are without result it is because it is difficult to get blood out of a stone. But as to the suggestion that he should make representations to the Governments of the United States and of the Swiss Republic, I need not say that if either of those Governments should think it right to make representations to Germany no one would be more rejoiced at or would welcome more heartily any steps of that kind than would the Government of this country. After all, it is not for us to dictate or even to suggest to the Governments of independent neutral countries what their duty is in such a case as this. It is for each Government to settle exactly what it ought to do with reference to foreign Governments, except so far as representations may be made on behalf of the subject of any other Government. Although I am quite ready to join with my hon. Friend in expressing the aspiration that these Governments may see their way to do something, if anything can be done, for the Armenians, I do not think it would be right that this Government should go further than that.

My hon. Friend said and said truly that it was not for us to make any representations to the Germans. It would be quite useless, and we certainly should not do so. But after all, they and they only are the people who can stop these massacres and can save the Armenians if they choose. I read in that very interesting and able pamphlet a statement that no sufficient proof of direct complicity can be brought against German officials, but indirectly the complicity of Germany is proved beyond doubt. Not only are they defended [by] Count Reventlow, but as I read in one of the German papers, beyond a communication from a German living in Switzerland, with that exception no protest of any sort or kind has appeared in any German paper. Not only so, it may sound a hard thing but it is true that the creed of German militarism leads logically to crimes of this description. Do not let us forget for a moment what a horrible thing, although it may be stated quite attractively, in reality German militarism is. It means that anything which is thought to be in the interests of the State is justified. The State is put in the place which is occupied in other nations by religion and morality. Once you grant that, once you grant that the so-called bastard patriotism is an excuse for any crime, there is no limit to the degradation of a nation that adopts such a belief as that. We in this country, I hope, will never accept such a doctrine.

We agree, at least I do with all my heart, with the words that Edith Cavell uttered just before her death:—

"Patriotism is not enough."

It is a thing which only a great patriot dare say, and she was one. It was said by a great patriot, and it is a profound truth that patriotism is not enough, and it is because the Germans have not realised but have denied that truth that they are accomplices even in this crime, and unless they abandon their idolatry they will sink even lower than they have sunk at present.

Major LANE-FOX: I hope the House will not think me at all disrespectful if after an absence for a considerable time I find it a little difficult to accommodate myself to what seems to be the rather unreal atmosphere in which we have spent this evening. I do not wish to say anything as to the want of reality of the three interesting speeches to which we have just listened, but in listening to them one could not help reflecting that unless, as the Under-Secretary of State for Foreign Affairs truly said, we can win this War, it is not very much use at the present moment discussing the Armenian Question, because for the moment we have lost all real control in dealing with it. Other subjects have been dealt with this evening. It is said the whole object of every man's ambition is to win the War. The only thing we think about at the front is how we are going to win this War, and it is rather difficult to come back and find this House jogging along with little differences of opinion, and Members not being prepared to combine and sink all those opinions to the one great object the men have before them... [continues on the topic of conscription]

ARMENIA.[*]

3. Mr. BIRD asked the Under-Secretary of State for Foreign Affairs whether a Report on the Turkish atrocities in Armenia has been written by Lord Bryce; and, if so, whether it will be laid before Parliament?

Lord R. CECIL: A valuable Report, consisting chiefly of a collection of documentary evidence, has been prepared at the suggestion of Lord Bryce by Mr. Arnold Toynbee, and will be laid before Parliament in due course.

ARMENIANS IN TURKEY. (MISCELLANEOUS, No. 31, 1916)[†]

Copy presented of Documents presented to Viscount Grey of Falloden, Secretary of State for Foreign Affairs, relating to the treatment of Armenians in the Ottoman Empire 1915-16, by Viscount Bryce, with a preface by Viscount Bryce [by Command]; to lie upon the Table.

RETURNS, REPORTS, &c.[‡]

Miscellaneous, No. 31 (1916)—The Treatment of Armenians in the Ottoman Empire, 1915-1916. Documents presented to Viscount Grey of Fallodon, Secretary of State for Foreign Affairs, by Viscount Bryce; with a Preface by Viscount Bryce:

Presented (by command) and ordered to lie on the Table.

ARMENIAN MASSACRES[**]
STATEMENT BY LORD R. CECIL

Mr. ANEURIN WILLIAMS (*by Private Notice*) asked the Secretary of State for Foreign Affairs whether His Majesty's Government have lately received any reports or information other than matter already published regarding the treatment accorded to the Armenian inhabitants of the Ottoman Empire during the present War?

Lord R. CECIL: His Majesty's Government have lately received information from a reliable source which gives much detailed evidence in regard to the systematic cruelties and outrages which have been inflicted on masses of Armenians who have been deported from their homes. The evidence goes to show that the Turkish officials have had recourse to various methods in order to exterminate these

[*] House of Commons, *Hansard* (5th series), Vol. LXXXV, 23 August 1916, col. 2650.

[†] House of Commons, *Hansard* (5th series), Vol. LXXXVII, 23 November 1916, col. 1547.

[‡] House of Lords, *Hansard* (5th series), Vol. LXXXV, 23 November 1916, col. 633.

[**] House of Commons, *Hansard* (5th series), Vol LXXXVIII, 21 December 1916, cols. 1636-37.

unfortunate people, that is, by famine, deliberate exposure to infectious disease, forced marches of aged men and women and young children, and, lastly, by massacres of gangs of labourers on pretext of insubordination.

Mr. WILLIAMS: Would the right hon. Gentleman have that information printed and circulated?

Lord R. CECIL: I will consider that. I think it will be possible, and I will certainly do it if it is.

Mr. T. P. O'CONNOR: May I ask the Noble Lord if he can trace any remonstrance by the German authorities against these massacres of the Armenians by the Turkish authorities?

Lord R. CECIL: No, Sir. As far as I know, no remonstrance has been made of any sort or kind.

Mr. O'CONNOR: Am I not right in saying that these massacres and other measures have been defended in official utterances in the German Reichstag?

Lord R. CECIL: I believe that they have been so defended, and there is no doubt whatever that the German Government had power to stop these outrages if they had chosen to do so, but they did not.

MASSACRE OF ARMENIANS

7. Sir EDWIN CORNWALL asked the Secretary of State for Foreign Affairs whether he has any official knowledge of the number of Armenians massacred; whether any communications have passed between the United States Government and the British

Government on the subject; and, if so, can he give any information to the House on these matters?

Lord R. CECIL: I am afraid that, owing to the circumstances of these massacres, it is impossible to obtain any official estimate of the number killed; nor have we received from or sent to the United States Government any communication on the subject. It is impossible, I fear, usefully to say anything further about these terrible events.

MOTION FOR ADJOURMENT[*]

War Situation: Prime Minister's Review...[†]

DAVID LLOYD GEORGE... These are the words I ventured to use with regard to Mesopotamia and the colonies [at a public speech in Glasgow]:

"What will happen to Mesopotamia must be left to the Peace Congress when it meets, but there is one thing which will never happen. It will never be restored to the blasting tyranny of the Turk. At best he was the trustee of this

---

[*] House of Commons, *Hansard* (5th series), Vol. C, 20 December 1917, col. 2220. The passage in question has been abridged from a significantly longer debate.

[†] Lloyd George's statements here were part of a wider debate on the war situation. We reproduce here his comments related to the Armenian issue.

far-famed land on behalf of civilisation. Ah, what a trustee! He has been false to his trust, and the trusteeship must be given over to more competent and more equitable hands, chosen by the Congress which will settle the affairs of the world. That same observation applies to Armenia, the land soaked with the blood of innocence, and massacred by the people who were bound to protect them."

That covers Mesopotamia. Now I come to the question of the colonies, and this is the statement which I then made.

"As to the German colonies, that is a matter which must be settled by the great International Peace Congress. Let me point out that our critics talk as if we had annexed lands peopled by Germans, as if we had subjected the Teutonic people to British rule. When you come to settle who shall be the future trustees of these uncivilised lands, you must take into account the sentiments of the people themselves—what confidence has been inspired in their untutored minds by the German rule, of which they have had an experience, whether they are anxious to secure the return of their former masters, or rather they would rather trust their destinies to other and juster, and—may I confidently say—gentler hands than those who have had the governing of them up to the present time. The wishes, the desires, and the interests of the people of these countries themselves must be the dominant factor in the settling of their future government."

Which of these two is challenged by hon. Gentlemen? Is it suggested that, whether the Arabs wish to return to Turkish rule or not, even if they are anxious not to, we shall hand them back; or that to the Armenians, who have gone through terror and massacre, we shall say, "In the interest of international morality and peace and goodwill amongst men, go back"; and as to the German colonies, about which tales are told that make one shudder, are we to say that these poor, helpless people, begging and craving, as they are doing, not to return them to German terrorism, "Yes, we will, whether you want it or not"? Is that the demand which is made? It is no use criticising unless we know what it is. What is it? The will of the people, the sentiments of the people—with the whites of Europe you have respected them, not with the poor blacks, not with the Arabs. ...

ARMENIA*

6. Sir RAMSAY MACDONALD asked the Secretary of State for Foreign Affairs if he is following the resistance which the Armenians are offering to the Turkish army seeking to overthrow the Armenian Republic in consequence of the declaration of that republic that it will not accept the provisions of the Brest-Litovsk Treaty regarding Armenia; and whether the Allied Governments pledge themselves to do everything in their power when the settlement after

* House of Commons, *Hansard* (5th series), Vol. 108, 12 November 1918, col. 473.

the War comes to be made that the future of Armenia will be decided upon the principle of self-determination?

Mr. BALFOUR: Yes, Sir, His Majesty's Government are following with earnest sympathy and admiration the gallant resistance of the Armenians in defence of their liberties and honour, and are doing everything they can to come to their assistance. As regards the future of Armenia, I would refer the hon. Member to the public statements made by leading statesmen among the Allied Powers in favour of a settlement upon the principle he indicates.

CONSOLIDATED FUND (APPRO-PRIATION) BILL*

Mr. ANEURIN WILLIAMS: The Leader of the House has reminded us that while Europe is to a large extent in revolution we in this country are in a comparatively happy position in spite of all the great sacrifices and sufferings endured during this War. I rise to ask the House to give a few minutes' attention to some parts of the world which are in an infinitely worse condition even than the greater part of the continent of Europe. I think it becomes us in our happy position to give a share of our thoughts to those unfortunate sufferers by the War. I desire to call attention to the condition

---

* House of Commons, *Hansard* (5th series), Vol. CXI, 18 November 1918, cols. 3239-3270. Aneurin William's discussion was part of a wider debate on military appropriations.

of the races that hitherto have been subject to Turkish misrule, and in particular to the Armenian race, and to the country called Armenia. The Armenians are a people of very great qualities who have suffered, no doubt, by their Eastern surroundings but of whom, by all the testimony I have been able to get, we may expect very great things from their abilities, industries, and their high qualities. They have suffered from time to time for generations from massacres and from every form of misrule at the hands of the Turks, and they have suffered especially because they were not content as a lower race might have been content, to live under Turkish misrule. They had aspirations and they desired reforms, and these were, in the eyes of their Turkish masters, their great offence.

They have suffered, too, from the inaction of the Great Powers. There was a time when Russia would have delivered them from Turkish misrule, but Great Britain would not allow it. There was also a time when Great Britain would have delivered them from Turkish misrule, Russia would not allow it; and there was a time when England and Russia both would have delivered them and Germany would not allow it. And so they have gone on from year to year, and generation to generation, now losing 30,000 in massacres, and then 50,000, and in the last few years it is estimated that they have lost 800,000 men, women and children in massacres since the beginning of this War— massacres, this last time, simply because they were believed to have sympathy with the Entente Powers—with ourselves and our Allies. The remnant of this race has fought magnificently in the mountains and in the desert places all through this War, and now, when the Armistice with Turkey has been signed, there are large numbers of refugees and deportees, men, women and children, who have been taken from their homes and put in concentration camps in the north of Syria and the higher parts of the Euphrates river.

The question arises, what is going to be done to save these refugees from famine and death? Up to now I have spoken only of the Armenians, but I do not desire to confine our sympathies or our charity or sense of duty simply to the Armenian race. The fund with which I am more particularly connected has, after all, confined itself to the Armenians, and it is called Armenian Refugees Lord Mayor's Fund. I am not suggesting that the sympathies of the people of this country should be confined to the people of the Armenian race, but they are the most prominent and the most suffering section, and they are the people connected with that great area which has been known from time immemorial as Armenia, and that is the area to which I desire to draw the attention of His Majesty's Government at the present time. The mass of refugees and deportees of all races and various religions in Asiatic Turkey is so great at present that to deal with them and save their lives is a problem which is entirely beyond the reach of private charity, and Government action is required. Government action, I believe,

is required in nearly all the lands which have been afflicted by the War in order to save the inhabitants of those lands from starvation. We know that in Europe the lands of our enemies, Germany and Austria, will require help if the people are to avoid starvation. We know that the lands of some of our allies, like Serbia, will require help no less than the Armenians, and that probably neutral territory, such as Holland, will require help in some way or another. This is almost a world-wide problem, and it certainly is one which extends over the greater part of Europe and a large part of the nearer Asia, and it is entirely beyond the reach of private charity.

I desire to call the attention of the Government to this question, and to ask what they are doing with this wide problem as it affects so many lands and so many races, and more particularly what they are doing in Asiatic Turkey and for the Armenian race. I know that all the private funds which have been started to deal with small parts of this great thing will not relax their efforts, but it is desirable that they should be co-ordinated, and they can only be adequately co-ordinated when the Government comes in and takes on the responsibility of doing what is absolutely necessary to save these people from starvation. These various funds can work together to do something more to re-establish these people in some degree of happiness and prosperity. I may say that so far from relaxing our efforts already, we have agents on the way out to the East in order to take up the work which has only just recently become possible. I am also informed of another fact to which I desire to call the Noble Lord's attention, and it is that large numbers of Armenians and other refugees are coming south from Asia Minor into the northern parts of Syria and Mesopotamia into the lands occupied by the British Army. We hear of 5,000 being found here, and 50,000 being found elsewhere, and the Army, I believe, is relieving them—indeed, I believe it is only the Army that has the power of relieving them at the present time. The mere fact of the absence of transport and organisation and civilian agencies connected with our Government and the French Government must make it a very difficult task to do anything immediately, and I am glad to believe that the Army has been doing so much in this matter. I would urge upon the Noble Lord that although the Army may step into the gap and do this work in the emergency which has arisen, there is much more needed than that. There is needed great organisation, and I think it can hardly be thought that it should be purely military organisation.

There is another thing. The Army is, of course, no longer opposing a powerful Army, and therefore it is only reasonable to suppose that the number of our Armies there instead of being increased will be rather diminished, and that certain units will be brought away, leaving only certain garrisons, and, of course, this will not increase the

transport facilities, and unless some other arrangements are made the effect will be that there will be less and less transport for bringing food to these destitute people, and the other necessaries to help them to re-establish themselves. I hope the Noble Lord will be able to tell us that the Foreign Office will see that by the withdrawal of troops on the instruction of the War Office nothing is done to diminish the transport and relieve distress in those regions. There is another very great difficulty, and that is the question of finance. I do not want to underrate that. We have, I know, calls upon us for great sums of money in all parts of the world at the present time, and to deal adequately with the distress which exists in Asiatic Turkey will undoubtedly need very considerable sums. I have no doubt that the United States of America and the French Government will be willing to take their part in finding the money necessary for this work. Of course, to arrange things between the three Governments concerned will necessarily take time, but I hope that there will be no delay allowed in doing the actual work. I am sure that we can trust our Allies to come in and do their part fully and generously, and in the meanwhile we ought to go on, being on the spot, pursuing this work with all the speed possible. I have no doubt that the Government is acting in this matter, and I only desire to have from the Noble Lord an assurance that it is so acting, and as much detail as he can give us of what they are doing in this matter.

And now I desire to pass from this very urgent question of saving the lives of these people to the question of the Government of the country known by the name of Armenia. We have been told several times that His Majesty's Government will not consent to the continuance of Turkish misrule over the subject races that they have hitherto rendered miserable. The word used was "misrule." I take it that when we were told that we would not consent to a continuance of Turkish misrule over this people, it meant that we should not consent to a continuance of Turkish rule in any form whatever, and not that hereafter they would be given Turkish reformed rule. I am sure that the Noble Lord will be able to tell us that there is no such meaning in the use of the word "misrule," and that we may reckon upon the total abolition of Turkish rule over the subject races in Asia Minor which have been rendered miserable so long by Turkish rule.

There is a point on which I should like further assurance, and on which I have more doubt. It is as to the question of Turkish suzerainty. I have no doubt that the Turks will try and maintain a suzerainty over these races, and particularly over the Armenians. I trust that His Majesty's Government and our Allies will not for one moment tolerate any such suggestion. No possible good could come from it, either for Turkey or anybody else, but much harm could come from it, because wherever Turkey has had the most shadowy form of suzerainty—as, for instance, in Egypt— it has used it to promote plots and

cabals, to try and get back its substantive power, and to reintroduce the tyranny from which those regions have been rescued. I trust that His Majesty's Government will not only see to the abolition of Turkish rule, but also to the abolition, root and branch, of Turkish suzerainty. I take it, therefore, that Armenia will be free from Turkish rule and Turkish suzerainty. I ask myself what the area will be. This is a matter of extreme importance. It is a matter of principle. We have fought this War in order to show that international right is enthroned as the supreme power among the nations, and in dealing with the Turkish Government I hope that we shall not forget that same great principle and great aspiration. I know it will be said that the country called Armenia has now comparatively few Armenians in it, but that remains to be seen. These people have immense courage and immense endurance, and many of them may have hid themselves in remote places in the mountains and have maintained themselves there during this War. They will come forth. Thousands of them have gone into Russia, into Persia, and into Egypt. They will come back to their homes. It does not at all follow that there will be only a small number of Armenians in Armenia when the whole account is cleared up. But, even if that were so, I make the strongest possible appeal to His Majesty's Government not to recognise that as a reason for limiting borders and the area of Armenia. To do so would be to put a premium upon massacre. To say that we will limit Armenia and, instead of taking in the whole of what was Armenia, that we will concentrate the Armenian races and only take in a small part, leaving the rest of the country to the Turks because the remainder of the people are largely Mahomedans, would be to put a premium upon massacre, and to tell the Turks, "You have been trying year after year to exterminate the Armenian people. You have succeeded so far that now we recognise that a large part of this area where the Armenians ought to be is only thinly inhabited by them, and we propose not to claim it as Armenia, but to concentrate the Armenian people and to leave this territory to you."

Armenia consists of the six vilayets, or provinces, up to the North-east of Asia Minor, and of the province of Cilicia, which is just the point where Syria and Asia Minor touch and which runs down to the Mediterranean. Those provinces constituted Greater and Lesser Armenia together. I plead that they should be constituted a State or a Government under some name or other, and that some one Power, as the mandatory of the Great Powers of the world, should be given a free hand to administer that area until such time as it is possible for them to have some form of self-government. A great part of the land from which the Armenians have been driven has been settled systematically by the Turks with Moslem immigrants. It has been going on during the War. That, however, is no reason why the country should be left under Turkish government. If the original owners of those lands are not to be found, I say nothing against leaving the Mahomedans in possession. I have no prejudice whatever against Mahomedans. We have an enormous number of Mahomedan citizens of this Empire, and they are happy and contented citizens. If good government is set up in Armenia, the Mahomedan people, however they came there, will benefit just as much as the Christian people. I ask that the whole area should be treated as one unit and that Cilicia should not be separated from the North-eastern vilayets. I will make one exception. There are certain parts of what is called Armenia which were added to the six vilayets by Turkey on purpose to create an artificial predominance of Mahomedan people over Armenians as a whole. They did not belong originally to the country called Armenia. They were inhabited by Kurds and other Mahomedan races, and they were tacked on in order to raise the percentage of Mahomedans and depress relatively the percentage of Armenians. Nobody would object to those purely Mahomedan districts being cut off, but, speaking of the six vilayets in their original and proper area, I plead very strongly that they and Cilicia should be treated as one unit and should be administered by some one of the great Powers, whether America, France, or ourselves, as the mandatory of all the Great Powers to establish there settled government and gradually train the people up to the point when they are able to govern themselves.

We ask for no privilege for any one race above the other races. We ask for equal rights for all civilised people. It is true that there will be great difficulties owing to the presence of certain nomadic and predatory tribes, which have been nomadic and predatory from time immemorial. It will be the task of those who are called upon to administer the country to confine those tribes to their own districts, and to see that no pillaging is allowed. When you have a separate Government set up in the country, Armenians will come back from Russia, from Persia, from America, from Egypt, from the Far East, and from all parts of the world, and they will settle again in the land of their fathers. All that work of repatriation will require a great amount of organising. It will be beyond the power of private charity or private effort to carry it out effectively, and I trust that we may have some promise from His Majesty's Government that they will use their power, their officials, and their soldiers to see that these people, coming back to the home of their fathers are settled upon the land in an orderly way, so that they may resume what has always been the great industry of the race, namely, agriculture, and once more cultivate and replenish that much-suffering land. I would remind my Noble Friend that when Greece was liberated from Turkey Turkish tyranny and Turkish massacres had reduced the population of that unhappy country to 400,000 people, as was estimated at the time. The population of the kingdom of Greece is now 5,000,000 people. That shows how a race will recuperate when once the deadly, blasting power of the Turk is removed and the people are given an opportunity of cultivating their land and pursuing their industries, refugees coming back from the uttermost parts of the world.

I should like to point out that there was much disappointment with regard to the terms of the Armistice,[*] because no provision was made for the occupation of any part of Armenia until such time as disorders arose. It would have been wiser to have taken precautions and to have occupied certain strategic points so as to see that no disorders did arise. To carry out the programme that I have sketched it would be necessary not only that certain points, but that the whole of the country should be occupied. I will merely sum up and say that I ask His Majesty's Government to recognise that this country owes a debt to Armenia, because, after all, we more than forty years ago prevented Armenia from being released by Russia from Turkish tyranny.[†] If we had not done that, the awful sufferings which have occurred since would not have occurred. We, therefore, owe them a debt. We owe them a further debt because they have fought valiantly for us in this War. In some measure to repay those debts, I ask that we should now organise the measures necessary to save the people

---

[*] Mudros Armistice.

[†] The reference is to Article 16 of the Treaty of San Stefano (1878), and Article 61 of the Congress of Berlin (1878).

from starvation, and that a little later on we should organise the measures necessary to enable them to come back methodically, safely and successfully to the land of their fathers that we should recognise Armenia as a great area not diminished by the policy of massacre, that we should administer the country by one of the great Powers as the mandatory of all the great Powers until such time as the people have been trained to manage their own affairs, and give another example of a free and prosperous nation.

Mr. BLISS: I should like to add a very [sic] words in support of what my hon. Friend has just said on this subject. I have no wish to reiterate the story of the sufferings of the Armenian people, but it seems to me that it is important that we should keep clearly in our minds some of the actual facts in order to understand the present position. We in England may perhaps, in a measure, realise what the sufferings of the Belgians have been during the occupation of their country by the Germans. They are Europeans, like ourselves. We can picture their weary marches along roads which are familiar to many of us. The case is absolutely different with regard to the Armenians in a distant country. It is only those who have climbed their mountains, traversed their valleys, who have lived amongst them in their huts, in their villages and their towns, and who know the people, who can realise how terrible their sufferings have been during recent years. What are the actual facts in this case? Early in 1915 the Armenian population

in the Turkish provinces amounted to something like 2,000,000 people, probably 1,800,000. In the spring of that year, under the administration of Enver Bey and Talaat Pasha, massacres and deportations were organised under a definite system, town following town in the visitation of their soldiery. In the first place, the young men in the village or town were summoned to the Government House, then marched out of the town, and there killed. The women who remained and the old men and children had a few days' grace; they were ordered to be deported, and they were deported. We must remember that any one of these women before deportation had the alternative offered to them of marching away into the unknown desert or of renouncing their faith and accepting Islam. To their great credit these women, though their bodies may have been polluted by their brutes of captors, preferred even that fate rather than renounce the faith of their fathers.

Some 600,000 of the people managed to evade the Turkish rulers, another 600,000, or possibly more, were deported and killed. There remain another 600,000 who were deported, and some of these are already, we believe, beginning to return. Some of them, we understand, have reached our lines, where they are all right and safe. Some of them are reaching the larger towns, where they may, or may not, find food, but many of them are seeking shelter in the ruins of their own hamlets and villages, and we know for a certainty that there starvation awaits them. No crops have been sown for a long time, the cattle have been driven away, there is no store of wheat or rice in the whole of the countryside, and there is nothing before these people but absolute want or absolute starvation. Since the War began food, even in the large seaboard towns, such as Constantinople and Smyrna, has been obtainable only at a prohibitive price, but during recent months, since Austria and Bulgaria ceased to traffic with Germany, many articles of food, such as tea, coffee, sugar and tinned provisions, have been absolutely unobtainable at any price. If that is the case in the large seaboard towns, what must it be in the remote country places? Again, the refugees who are slowly returning to their old homes are subject to the molestation and ravage of the demobilised and discharged soldiery. We have heard, during the War, a good deal about the "Clean fighting Turk." That may or may not be the case, but there is certainly very little that is clean about the discharged Turkish soldier who is wandering at large throughout the country, especially when he is dealing with helpless and poverty-stricken people. The old lands of these people, who are coming back, have been taken possession of by the Turks. I remember how after the Turkish War the Moslem refugees were planted in Anatolia at various places and occupied the lands of the dispossessed farmers, who have no means of sustenance left. It is the utter misery and the desolate condition of these people that call aloud to England to come to their rescue at

the present time. We must also remember the gallant help which the Armenians gave us in the course of this War. I believe they maintained and equipped considerable forces entirely at their own expense, and they did splendid service in fighting against the Turks in the Eastern parts of Asia Minor. I believe that the capture of Erzerum and Trebizond were greatly due to their efforts. They held back the Turks in the Caucasus right up to the capture of Batoum. Many Armenians were found in the Russian ranks; they are fighting in Poland, and they are also in considerable numbers in our British Armies, in the American Armies, and in the French Armies at the front. I have little knowledge of military affairs, but it seems to me that as Belgium was made the highroad for the Germans into France, and as Serbia was the corridor of their great Berlin to Bagdad route, so Armenia and the Caucasus formed the highway in the direction of Central Asia and on to the frontiers of India.

With regard to the future, I dislike intensely the term "Buffer State," but at the same time I think it is essential that a free, strong, and preferably a Christian state should be established in Armenia and in the Caucasus. I know quite well the difficulties of establishing such a State where the population is so mixed, consisting as it does of Armenians, Turks, Kurds, Tartars, and other races, but, in view of the recent Turanian movement, it is essential to future peace that an independent State should be established between the Turks in

Anatolia in the West and the other races more to the East speaking the same language, having a common religion with the Turks. We need a State between them to safeguard the future of Central Asia and also to safeguard the highway to the Northern Frontiers of India itself. England, with all its traditions of sympathy for the oppressed and suffering nations, cannot afford at this time to turn a deaf ear to the cry that is coming to her from this remnant of a nation. What should be the method for the future? I venture to suggest what appears to me to be the correct solution, that a small force be sent to occupy the strategic points or the principal points in that region, say, five or six different places—Trebizond, Erzerum, Kars, Ourfa, Diarbekir, and Van. If you sent, so far as the terms of the Armistice permit, a small force to occupy those centres, they would not only safeguard the remnant of the Armenians who are returning to their homes, but they could administer relief work and form a nucleus or a starting-point for the future settlement of the country. I hope that for these reasons the Government will give us some assurances on the matter to-night.

Sir GEORGE GREENWOOD: As this is the last occasion on which I shall have an opportunity of addressing this House, I hope Members will bear with me if I say a few words on a subject in which I have always felt very great interest. Ever since the years 1879-80 I have always, when opportunity allowed and to the best of my poor ability, advocated that it should be the main principle of our foreign policy, and its ultimate principle, that the Ottoman Turk should be expelled from Europe and also from any territory in Asia, if it might be and when the possibility arose, where he held sway over Christian communities. I did not advocate that on the ground that the Turk is a Mahomedan and that these subjects were Christians. We know that the Mahomedans in some places,—for instance, the Moors in Spain—have been able to make excellent governors, but the Mahomedan Turk comes of the Tartar race, and history has amply proved that he is unable to afford even the semblance of a decent government to the Christian races subordinate to him. His rule has been called "an organised brigandage." I would call it:

"The abomination of desolation . .
. . . standing where it ought not."

Eleven years ago, when in this House we were discussing the Macedonian question, I used the following words:

"I only wish we could say with Mr. Gladstone, let the Turks now carry off their abuses in the only possible way, namely, by carrying off themselves—let them go bag and baggage. . . . That is the ultimate object which we have in view. . . Anybody who at this time of day places faith in Turkish promises is blind to all the teaching of history."

I am afraid that some hon. Members even then placed faith in Turkish promises, for I find that, speaking on the Appropriation Bill of that year, 1907, the hon. Member for East Nottingham (Sir J. D. Rees), who I believe considers himself a high authority on matters of the East I would like to appeal, and who was then Liberal Member for the Montgomery Boroughs, took me severely to task for what I said then. I am sorry the hon. Member is not in his place to hear me, but as I was absent when he criticised me on that occasion, there is no inequality. He said:

> "The hon. Member for Peterborough the other night had expressed the strongest anti-Turkish feeling, which was so common and so frequently expressed in that House. He wished that this subject was more calmly and more temperately considered. In point of fact, it was of the greatest importance to us. We actually had more Mahomedan subjects than the Sultan of Turkey, who was regarded by Mahomedans with the greatest respect and veneration, and almost worship. It was most desirable that the Sultan should be spoken of with respect in discussing these matters, and the dislike which some had to him ought at least to be dissembled. He did not share that dislike himself."

Those were words spoken of Abdul Hamid, who had been branded by Mr. Gladstone as the "great assassin," and who was generally known as "Abdul the Damned." He was the friend of the Kaiser; he fraternised with the German Kaiser and became on good terms with the Kaiser, and they were seen walking arm in arm together. I see the hon. Member added:

> "He was acquainted with the Mahomedans and their languages, and he believed them to be on the whole a most excellent race."

One lives and learns. I had always thought that Mahomedan was a term that denoted religion and not race. However, we are told otherwise on the great authority of the hon. Member. At any rate, he has learnt that Mahomedan Indians and Mahomedan Arabs are perfectly willing to fight for the British Empire against the Ottoman Turk though they are a Mahomedan Power.

Then, coming to the broad question of Armenia, we remember those terrible massacres in 1895 and 1896, but they pale into insignificance before what has been done during this War. The Germans have been guilty of the most ghastly and unspeakable crimes, but there is no crime so ghastly and unspeakable as the wholesale massacre, under circumstances of the greatest possible barbarity and atrocity, of the Armenians. One feels that this country has a great amount of responsibility in this matter, because we were responsible for the Treaty of Berlin and for the Cyprus Convention, and we were responsible for handing back the Armenians to the Turks under a treaty with very similar conditions to that of Brest-Litovsk. The question is, of course, what is to be done in the future? It is clear that no faith whatever is to be placed upon any promise given by the Turks. I suppose it will be universally accepted that the Turkish rule in Armenia must be for ever gone. It has been suggested that there should be an

Armenian State, consisting of the six vilayets and Cilicia, under the protection of the Allied Great Powers, one of them acting as the mandatory of all the Powers, for a term of years, at any rate, in order to organise and to administer that State. That is a question which will be considered by high authorities when peace comes to be settled. I believe it is a term of the Armistice that if there are disorders in Armenia the Allies should send in troops to occupy part of that territory. I do not know how far it is true, but we are told that there are and have been great disorders, and the Turks joining the Tartar troops, which are their kith and kin, are in certain places still trying to pursue the old Turkish policy, which was to kill the Armenian question by killing the Armenian nation. If that is so, I hope we shall be able, if measures have not already been taken, to put a stop to that by sending troops into the country. I believe it is true that if it had not been for the stout resistance of the Armenians during this War the Turks might have overrun Persia and they might have turned the flank of the British armies in Mesopotamia. Therefore, for every reason in history and for every reason arising out of this War, we stand committed to the miserable remnant of the Armenians and I think there are a great many more than people contemplate, because there is a large number in Transcaucasia, who will come back when security is established. I hope the Noble Lord will be able give to us an assurance that if these rumours are true and these Turkish outrages are continuing in certain parts of Armenia, troops may be sent in to occupy the country. I think we owe that to Armenians, and we owe it to justice.

Major PEEL: I shall say nothing about massacres. Let the simple consideration suffice that, long as human history has lasted and long as it will last, no crimes are so execrable or, I hope, will be so execrable, as the recent atrocities in Armenia. Nor shall I refer to the terms of the recent Armistice, though in some respects it was unfortunately drawn so that under Article 24 there has been created a sense of acute disquietude among the friends of Armenia on the ground that the state of that country seems very disturbed at present, and it will be long before peace can arise and the atrocities be stopped. We shall be very glad indeed to have some assurance from the Noble Lord which will satisfy our anxieties on that point. What I wish to deal with principally is the future organisation of Armenia. It seems to me that that depends entirely upon our whole policy in the near East, and that in its turn really hinges on the question of who is to be master at Constantinople. In January 1917, we had a most satisfactory statement on that matter on behalf of the Allies. It was stated on that occasion that the civilised world knows that part of the Allied aims is the turning out of Europe of the Ottoman Empire as decidedly foreign to Western civilisation. That was most satisfactory from the point of view which I share. But that agreeable prospect was entirely upset at the start of this year in a speech by the Prime Minister expressing the war aims of this country and, I suppose, of other countries when he said:

"Nor are we fighting to deprive Turkey of the rich and renowned lands of Asia Minor which are predominantly Turkish in race."

He seemed to attach so much importance to making things quite clear on that point that later on, in the same speech, he said:

"We do not challenge the maintenance of the Turkish Empire in the homelands of the Turkish race centring on its capital of Constantinople."

Therefore, it is absolutely clear that as long as the existing declared policy of the Government stands, the Turks are not to be turned out, and the Turkish power is to remain centred in what the Prime Minister described as the homelands of the race centring on Constantinople.

I really felt when I read that utterance—I did not for patriotic reasons criticise it during the course of the War—that one would almost explain, in the words of Lord Beaconsfield, when he came back from the Treaty of Berlin, "Turkey in Europe exists once more." Therefore, it seems to me that we are pledged, so far, not to disturb the corrupt camarilla of Constantinople, not to disturb that cesspool of Levantine corruption, that focus of Turkish intrigue. If that is so, it appears to me to have two direct and very painful results for our whole policy in the Near East. In the first place, if

you look at Arabia, we are trying to foster the power and influence of the King of the Hedjaz, the Shereef of Mecca. We are trying to start and organise, rightly, what I may call a pan-Arabian policy as opposed to the pan-Islamism of the Committee of Union and Progress. Or else one might say, viewing it from the ecclesiastical standpoint, that we are weaning Sunnite Islam, from the Ottoman school. But I am afraid if we are going to leave the Turkish party of Union and Progress in control at Constantinople that policy is a dream. We shall find that, for all our efforts, we shall be doing nothing more than to establish in Arabia an Arabian pontiff, half buried in the Arabian sands. But if the rest of our Near Eastern policy is to establish a certain number of young independent races and bring them into the status of nations, as long as you leave a focus of Turkish intrigue and Turkish influence predominant at Constantinople, so long the lives of those young independent nations, such as Armenia, are impossible, and your policy is a dream. There are very powerful influences of international finance which are in favour of the continuation of those forces at Constantinople. But I am glad to think that there are no statesmen so competent, and I believe so ready, to combat those influences and to deal with that matter as the right hon. Gentleman (Mr. Balfour) and the Noble Lord (Lord R. Cecil). Therefore I should be very glad if we can have some pronouncement on the question that I have raised so far.

I should like to consider for a few minutes what might be the organisation of Armenia, and perhaps I might preface what I say with the remark that I consider no satisfactory settlement of the Armenian question possible as long as the question of Constantinople remains unsatisfactory. The first point, I think, is, a great many people say that Armenia is wiped out, and, therefore, there is no Armenian question at all. As far as I can judge, there were about 1,800,000 in Asiatic Turkey before the War. Six hundred thousand have been massacred, 600,000 have become Moslems or are hiding in the country, Catholic or Protestant Armenians who have not been hurt, and the other 600,000 are exiles. It seems to me, therefore, that there is a nucleus of Armenians, and we may reckon on 1,200,000 Armenians who might form, I think, a very satisfactory nucleus for the reconstituted state of Armenia. I should just like to add that, as far as I can judge, in the six vilayets there were about 400,000 Kurds. Some of those Kurds, I think, have been wiped out in the course of this struggle, and therefore I see no reason why the Armenians, if they come back, should not be able to settle their State satisfactorily. The first risk which Armenia runs I have now dealt with. The second risk is that she may be divided up into parts. In particular, I should like to have an assurance on that point. Some hon. Gentlemen may smile at the possibility of such a thing happening, but still we have to recall, when we read the Memorandum of March, 1917,

published by the Bolshevists, that in the spring of 1916 there was a secret treaty entered into between France, Britain and Russia, I think, for the actual division of Armenia. I think, though I do not, perhaps, burden my memory quite accurately, that the terms implied that Russia was to have the vilayets of Erzerum, Bitlis, and Van. The remaining portion of Armenia, from Adana and Alexandretta up to the Russian border of the new State, was to be in the hands of France. Therefore the second risk I see facing the Armenians is that it may be divided up into parts as it was done in the secret treaty. I am sure from what the Noble Lord has said that this country always keeps all its treaties, but I should be glad to hear that we did not regard that one as of vital importance. There is a third risk, I think, facing the new Armenian State that we hope to float, and that is that it may be formed into what is called a Milet. Those who have read the history of Turkey know that Milets started with the great Sultan Mohammed II. He organised the races of Turkey under ecclesiastical control, and the nation he formed under the disguise of a Church, and only yesterday I was reading a proposal of a very great friend of Armenia that the Armenians should in future be organised in the same way.

I contend that there are tremendous obstacles to that. In the first place, they would have no territorial position; they would have an entire separation of peoples. They would have no geographical position, and, above all, they would have no executive power, and, having no executive power, they would have no safety. They would become, if I may venture to recall a phrase of Bismarck—they would become a bubble in the Near Eastern lake. I hope we may hear from the Noble Lord that that is not in the mind of the Government. There is one further solution also that has been proposed about which I should like to say a word. It is the solution of the Turkish question which was associated, I think, with the policy of the Sultan Mahmud II., who ruled in the early part of the nineteenth century. His plan was to amalgamate all the various races of Turkey under one central government. That policy was pursued by those who came after him and has a great deal to recommend it still, for whereas to some parts of the Turkish Empire it could not be applied—to the Rumanians, Greeks, and Bulgars, all of whom are hopelessly Irredentists from the Turkish point of view—it might well apply conceivably to a race like the Armenians who are indissolubly connected in some respects with Turkish industry, finance and the whole life of the Turkish State, and are scattered in some places far and wide throughout the country. I contend, though there are powerful arguments in favour of that solution, that policy has been absolutely destroyed by forty years' government of Abdul Hamid. That man set himself to destroy the policy of Mahmud. He set race against race, and what was started by him was completed in our own age by Talaat Pasha—Abdul was the Metternich, Talaat was the Marat—of the Near East. There

remains one more solution of the Armenian question, and that is the guarantee of Europe. When I say that there comes up before me a host, a whole series, of broken and violated guarantees. There was the Treaty of San Stefano which was torn up at Berlin. There was the futile Berlin Treaty of 1878. There was the collective note of the Powers in 1880 that was flung in their faces. There was the agreement of 1895, which was never carried out, and there was the futile Constitution of 1908. There was the still more futile agreement of 1914, which was blown to pieces on the outbreak of the European War, and last of all I may add, an agreement which must also be made futile, the Secret Treaty of 1916. In face of that whole host and series of European guarantees can we hope for anything from the concert of Europe? We can hope for nothing unless we can carry out the work with which the Noble Lord on the bench opposite is so honourably associated—I mean that we turn the Concert of Europe into the League of Nations, for, however futile the arrangements of the Concert of Europe were, at least we may say there was in them a certain element of good will.

We wish that good will to be rendered strong and organised by the collected will of humanity, as expressed in that great policy. There is one question that will still have to be asked: Suppose the League of Nations is established, and these new nations are set up in the Near East, are they to be protected by many Powers or by one?

Well, we have had enough of international control. We have seen too much of it in Egypt, and therefore it would be far better to have one Power, the mandatory of Europe in Armenia. Shall that Power be England? I very much hope not, though I very much look forward to the time when she will be the mandatory in Mesopotamia. Shall that Power be France? We cannot expect it of her now that her resources are exhausted and the power of her race cut off. Shall it be one of the Balkan States? I feel sure the great statesman of Greece, M. Venizelos, is far too prudent to wish to take up that great task. Shall it be Bulgaria? No! As for Serbia and Roumania, their hands are too full. There is only one Power that remains. It is that Power which for a generation past has instilled into Armenia the ideas of hope and progress—I mean the United States of America. I recall the fact that so long as twenty-two years ago I had the honour, if I may be excused a personal reminiscence, of speaking with the late Mr. Gladstone at Hawarden. That was in September, 1898. I think it was in August, 1896, that there had culminated those terrible atrocities in Armenia which had swept away 100,000 of the Armenian race. I came to see the great statesman on another subject, but I found that he was entirely absorbed in the thought of Armenia. He told me that just as when a young man his interests had been absorbed in the freedom of Italy so in his old age he felt the first obligation upon him was toward the martyred people of Armenia. He added a phrase which I think I can repeat, "That of all the nations of the world no history has been so blameless as the history of the Armenian people." I conclude where I started, that the root of the question and the issue in this matter is this, Who is to be the master at Constantinople, and whether it is to be the corrupt camarilla which has so long disgraced it or whether it is to be some purer and better influence? I hope that we may have some more satisfactory assurance on that matter than was announced to us in January of this year, for in that lies the very core and root of the matter, and is, if I may, in conclusion, adapt or adopt the phrase of the old Roman statesman, *articulus stantis aut cadentis Armenioe.*

Sir J. SPEAR: I beg the indulgence of the House to address to it the last words which I shall be privileged to speak in this Chamber, after many years' service in it, and to give ardent support to the speeches which have been delivered appealing to the Government that in the settlement that is to be made with regard to Turkish affairs Turkey shall have no further influence or power in the government of Armenia. On behalf of my Constituents I wish to say that they have gladly borne the tremendous sacrifices of the War and borne their share towards this great War for liberty and for the interests of civilisation and justice which has ended so triumphantly; but if Turkey is allowed to retain any power over Armenia I am sure my Constituents would be deeply disappointed. Tragedies have occurred throughout the War and tortures have been committed, but nothing moved my people more than the action of Turkey in taking thousands of Armenians out to sea and throwing them into the water to drown. For very many years this tragedy of the massacre of Armenians has again and again recurred, and it is time in the interests of humanity that it should cease. Though I doubt not the Government are equally desirous of protecting the Armenians, I venture most respectfully, on behalf of those I represent, to say that if a vestige of power is retained by Turkey over Armenia they will be disappointed. With reference to Turkey, I would like to see the principle advocated by Mr. Gladstone put into force, namely, that Turkey should be turned, bag and baggage, out of Europe. I am not a sufficient judge of high politics to dogmatically express an opinion upon that point, but the more the power of Turkey is limited the better it will be for humanity. I should like to say a word of high appreciation of the action of our Government with regard to Palestine. British people glory in the recovery of that land from the hands of the Turks, and we appreciate very highly the action of the Government in giving encouragement to the Jews to return to their own land, and I earnestly hope that their powers will be used still further in that direction.

A word with reference to the League of Nations. We do not want a recurrence of this terrible War. We know it is a very difficult problem, and I have every confidence in the Government that they will do their best to solve it in the interests of the world;

but we cannot help thinking, those of us who have a limited knowledge of high politics, that when the Allied nations have bound themselves together and made their sacrifices of blood and treasure to win this War, that the same combination could be so modelled as to prevent a recurrence of such a disaster as this War. I feel sure that the present circumstances are of a peculiarly fitting and opportune character for the accomplishment of that purpose. I know quite well from statements we have had from prominent members of the Government that they will not lose sight of this important development. With even our limited and humble knowledge we know that there are considerable difficulties in the problem, but we shall feel that we have failed to accomplish all that we have striven for in this War unless a league is established which will prevent a recurrence of this disaster and tragedy. I should like to add, in regard to Armenia, that after the massacre of something like 600,000 Christians in that country, for no fault except that the Turks wished to annihilate the nation, we have a right to expect from the Government that not one vestige of power should be allowed to remain in the hands of those who have proved themselves quite incapable of dealing fairly and considerately with any peoples under their rule.

Mr. HUGH LAW: It has been one of the noblest traditions of the party to which I have the honour to belong that for many years they have associated themselves on every occasion with the cause of freedom in all lands, and it would not be fitting for this Debate to end without a voice, however feeble, being raised from these benches. I cannot pretend to that knowledge which many of my friends have of foreign politics or such knowledge as would enable me either to propound or to criticise particular policies and particular solutions. I desire quite simply to ask the right hon. Gentleman the Assistant Secretary for Foreign Affairs a simple question, which even the most ignorant of us may well ask and to which I think we have a right to expect an answer. The Government spokesman, intentionally or unintentionally, have used, in relation to the continuance of Turkish rule, words which are at least capable of two interpretations. In a recent answer given to me, the Foreign Secretary said that it had always been a principal purpose of His Majesty's Government to put an end to Turkish misrule in Armenia. That is an admirable saying, and I have no doubt a true one, but one cannot but remember that exactly the same phrase has been used before on many occasions, and that it has not, in fact, prevented a recurrence of such horrors as have been alluded to by the Mover of this Resolution and other speakers. I want the Noble Lord to say quite plainly whether or not, when he speaks of ending Turkish misrule, he does mean ending Turkish rule. I think it is really right that we should know quite plainly and simply whether that is so. It is true that in a certain sense, and a very profound sense, the two things are the same, because Turkish rule has always

been misrule and the phrase, "ending Turkish misrule," has so often covered the continuance of that very rule.

I do not believe that anyone at this time of day can desire that the Turk should continue as a governor over any subject people. The Turk has many virtues. The Turkish peasant is said by those who know him to be among the most honest, kindly and hard-working of mankind, and the Turkish soldier is said to fight cleanly and as a gentleman. I do not know whether that is always so, but certainly for the Turkish Government, as distinct from the rest, there is nothing to be said. The rule of the Turk in every one of the countries he has ruled has been a curse. All of us, I suppose, without exception, has borne during the last four years a load of personal anxiety, and we have never known for a moment when a chance shot might not bring down into the dust all that we have loved. But we have been buoyed up by this thought, that those in regard to whom we bore that anxiety were fighting to bring to an end the tyranny in the world. That task, so far as Western Europe is concerned, is happily accomplished. Do not, I beg of you, allow it to remain where the most ancient and most corrupt evil of all times has cursed some of the fairest lands in the world.

Mr. PONSONBY: I should like to join with those who have spoken in expressing the hope that at last the unfortunate people of Armenia will find a country in which they can dwell in security. I do not think there is any people throughout the world who have suffered as these unfortunate people have suffered. My hon. Friend, who sits by me, has in a very interesting speech referred to the various futile attempts that have been made to correct Turkish misrule in that part of the world. If in peace time, when the concert of Europe by way of working together in harmony was quite unable to deal with this problem, quite unable to establish a state of affairs that would enable the Armenian people to live under tolerable conditions, it does make one a little apprehensive, seeing the turmoil in which the world is placed to-day, whether greater success will attend the efforts of Powers. I feel confident that the rule of the Turk is one that can no longer be tolerated over subject races of non-Ottoman nationality in that part of the world. As my hon. Friend (Mr. Hugh Law) said, it is not the Turkish soldier, it is not the Turkish peasant, but it is the Turkish Government that is corrupt and cannot be trusted. I well remember that in my maiden speech in this House made eleven years ago, I expressed grave doubts as to the success of what was then known as the Turkish Revolution. I did not trust the Turk as a governor, and in successive years we have seen that this failure has become more and more pronounced. In 1895 I was in Constantiople, and there was great rejoicing that the Concert of Europe and the ambassadors representing that Concert had got Sultan Abdul Hamid to agree to a scheme of Armenian reform. Abdul Hamid was one of the most subtle and most astute diplomatists who were ever

in Europe. He knew exactly the moment when to put a spoke into the wheel of the machine of the Concert and make the various Powers fall out with one another. He would agree to reforms without having the smallest intention of carrying them out. One of the stipulations at that time was that wherever a vilayet contained a Christian majority, that vilayet should have a Christian governor and administrator. Very shortly afterwards Abdul Hamid took care to see that there was no Christian majority in any vilayet by the means which he always himself, from his Palace at Yildiz, employed—that of massacre. We want no ambiguity or doubt as to the future of these people. As regards the other peoples in the Near East, there may be contests between various Powers as to who will have this bit of territory and who will have that. I look forward to these questions with misgiving, but with regard to Armenia, humanity in all nations would agree that at all events their grievances should be redressed.

As the Noble Lord (Lord Robert Cecil) the representative of the Foreign Office is here, I should like to raise one question which is of extreme gravity. I think that within two days of the end of the Session, and with an appeal to the country before us, we ought to have a very clear statement from the Government as to what our policy is with regard to Russia. It is most unfortunate that at this moment information should be withheld from us as to what our Expedition in the North of Russia is actually doing, what our intention is towards the Bolshevik Government, and whether reinforcements, and considerable reinforcements, are being sent to that part of the world. I was surprised at the amount of feeling which exists in the country on this subject. At meetings which I have addressed recently I had constant questions from the audience as to what our policy in Russia is and when our Expedition in Russia is going to be withdrawn. I do not want to go back over the ground of our attitude towards the Russian Revolution. It was a most unfortunate attitude. If we had supported the great movement that overthrew Czardom, we might have evolved out of it a form of democracy which would have been of immense value as a model to the world. But we gave it the cold shoulder, and not content with that, and at a time when we have witnessed the sentiments that have come from the Russian revolution spreading like a forest fire and going all over the countries, and when thrones are falling, and sparks of the fire are reaching even to the very far West—not content with witnessing the devastating effects of what is termed "Bolshevism," we actually, according to rumour—and according to rumour which seems to have a very good foundation—have continued to stir up by our action in Russia sentiment against the Bolshevik Government. I really think that now, when there is an Armistice with the Central Powers, now when peace has come and there is a cessation of hostilities, if the people believe that our soldiers will be sent out to the Arctic regions in winter for the sake of stirring up strife against a Government which, however much we disagree with it, is in the saddle, and is conducting a transition stage in Russia with the greatest difficulty, the indignation of our people will be very great. Whatever mistakes the Russian people may be making, let them work out salvation for themselves without interference from outside, and I hope that the Noble Lord will now that we have so little time left before the end of the Session, give some information in order to allay these fears which exist, and, if he can tell us that the Government have decided upon the withdrawal of the Expedition from Russia, there would be no more welcome news in the country to-day.

The UNDER-SECRETARY of STATE for FOREIGN AFFAIRS (Lord Robert Cecil): The concluding observations of the hon. Member for Stirling raise a matter which I am the first to admit is one of the most immense importance, but on which it is peculiarly difficult for me to speak, because it involves not so much diplomatic as military considerations. The hon. Member himself will see that it is quite impossible for me to give any pledges or undertakings as to what our military action is or is not going to be in Russia, without, at any rate, having previous consultation with those who are responsible for military operations in that country.

Mr. PONSONBY: We are not at war with them?

Lord ROBERT CECIL: I did not say we were. I said that there were military operations.

Colonel WEDGWOOD: What are they—military operations between the Foreign Office and the War Office?

Lord R. CECIL: This I can say, that the Government are fully aware of the considerations which the hon. Member has put forward, and have got them very much in their minds, and they are certainly not disposed to entangle this country at the close of a great war in serious military operations. Beyond that I cannot go, and I confess I should have heard the hon. Member's speech with more agreement had I heard in it some condemnation of the really outrageous proceedings of the so-called Government in Russia. It is not only their great offence against humanity and good government, which the hon. Member may think is mainly a matter for the Russians themselves; but after all they have committed offences against this country which, if they had been committed by any ordinary civilised Government, would have more than justified this country in seeking redress by arms. After all, they have killed without justification one of our naval officers in Petrograd who was doing his duty—protecting the Embassy from entry by unauthorised persons. That is only one of the many things which they have done.

Mr. KING: We had not any Embassy.

Lord R. CECIL: That is a perfectly irrelevant observation—and not only so, but the circumstances were of a really horrible character. There are many British subjects in Moscow and Petrograd against whom they have committed other crimes which really, to use a celebrated phrase, might "stagger humanity." Therefore, although I think that we are bound to consider and ought to consider primarily the interests and desires of the people of this country, yet when we are dealing with this subject, it is right to say that the Bolshevik Government as such is entitled to no consideration whatever from the British Government.

I pass now to the subject which formed the main topic this afternoon. It is not necessary for me to express on behalf of the Government the profound agreement with which I heard the expression of sympathy with the Armenian people, and the damnation of the incredible outrages to which they have been submitted by the Turks, both recently and before. Of course we recognise the tremendous claims that the Armenians have from every point of view on the assistance and protection of this country as well as of other civilised countries in Europe, and, if I do not enlarge on the horrors which have been enacted there and on the sufferings through which the Armenians have gone, it is not for want of sympathy, but because the subject is so very well known, and I trust that the sentiments of the British Government are equally well known on that subject.

There are three broad questions which have been put to me. First, I was asked whether we would agree, in order to relieve the immediate wants of the

Armenians, to take any steps to feed these starving Armenian people and provide for their pressing necessities. My hon. Friend who raised this question at the beginning of the Debate will recognise that it is a big and difficult question. Almost the whole world is crying out for food and assistance, and we have to consider the claims of all these people together, and as being part of one great subject. The relief of hunger and distress all over the world is one of the subjects which are preoccupying his Majesty's Government most of all at the moment. As far as Armenia is concerned, the Government hope that the military authorities will be able to do something immediately. In addition to that the Food Commission, which is an international or inter-Allied body, and represents the Allies, has been charged with and is now considering the question of how the Government can provide for the feeding of these populations most effectively. I cannot say exactly what they have done yet, but no doubt they are taking all possible steps, and I know that Armenia has been brought to their notice prominently as one of the first claims to their consideration. I am afraid I cannot add anything to that. The matter is one which must take time and must be developed in connection with other populations. There are many other districts, Poland and other places, which must be considered at the same time.

I was asked what measures have been completed, or were about to be taken, for the protection of the Armenian people immediately apart from its future government. Some criticism was made of the terms of the Armistice. There has been, I think, a good deal of misapprehension on this subject. In the first place, provision has been made for the repatriation of the Armenians at present imprisoned or interned by the Turks, and in that matter the Armenians have been singled out from all the other races and have been put upon the same terms as our own prisoners of war. I have forgotten the exact terms, but I think that by Clauses 5 and 16 of the Armistice provision is made. By Clause 5 there is provision for the withdrawal generally of Turkish forces beyond those actually required to maintain order from the district of Cilicia. That matter ought not to be forgotten, and in order to be quite sure that the Turks will not be able to return, all railway connection between Armenia and Constantinople will be cut off altogether; and I think it is an important matter from this point of view to keep the Turkish soldier, as far as possible, outside of Armenia. Once you are in possession, at least so I am told, of the most important strategic position of Cilicia, you effect that and that strategic point is to be occupied without delay as is provided, I think, by Clause 10 of the Armistice. In addition to that there is the general power to occupy strategic points wherever a situation arises which threatens the security of the alliance. It is quite plain therefore, that if there were anything like disorder and disturbance it would be within the power of the Allied powers to occupy any strategic points.

Sir G. GREENWOOD: Is it not the fact that the Turks are now maltreating the Armenians there?

Lord R. CECIL: If that be so, no doubt action will be taken. I have no information that that is so beyond what we have seen in the public Press. In the Clause to which I have just referred, there is power—and a power which I am quite sure will be exercised as far as military considerations permit—to occupy any necessary positions in Armenia. Those are the main principles with regard to the immediate protection of the Armenians. I can assure the House that in this matter the Government is deeply in earnest. They feel, I hope, the demands of humanity, and, quite apart from those demands, they feel that they would expose themselves, and rightly expose themselves, to the indignation of the country if they allowed further atrocities to take place in Armenia when they had the power to prevent them by military means.

There were two or three interesting and important questions about the future government of Armenia. One hon. Member said that the root of the matter was the ejection of Turkish government from Constantinople. I quite admit that there is a great deal to be said for that, but at the same time my hon. Friend will not forget that after all Constantinople is predominantly Turkish. That is a thing which must be considered in dealing with this subject, if we are not to be false to all the professions which we have made on these questions.

Mr. A. WILLIAMS: Can the right hon. Gentleman say that there are 50 per cent. of Turks in Constantinople?

Lord R. CECIL: I am informed that there are more than 50 per cent. There is a number of Greeks, Ottoman Greeks, and Greek Greeks, but I think most authorities, at any rate, put the Turks in a majority. I do not suppose there have been any accurate statistics. My hon. Friend quoted the declaration made by the Prime Minister in January of this year. I have not got, I am sorry to say, the words of that declaration before me. I think I may say that was an international declaration made by the Prime Minister, speaking for the British Government, but many things have occurred since then, and I do not at all think that this Government is bound by the letter of that declaration.

It would not be right for me to go further—the matter must be considered at the Peace Conference. It is not right for the British Government to go into the Peace Conference saying beforehand on a matter of this kind, a matter of very great interest, "This is the solution which we have prepared and which we intend to have, and before even we have had the opportunity of discussing it with our Allies." But they have a free hand, and are not bound to any solution. I think everyone will agree that whatever be done, two things are quite certain: We cannot let those evil forces which have been predominant in Constantinople remain predominant as the predominant Government in Constantinople; and we must secure that the Dardanelles and the Bosphorus are absolutely free. As a matter of fact, the forts of the Bosphorus are, I believe, at this moment under the control of the Allied forces. My hon. Friend will recognise that, if we can go straight through to the Black Sea, the actual technical sovereignty of Constantinople becomes of less importance. You can get the great power of Constantinople from its geographical situation. That is the main point—to shut off all approach from the Black Sea and the countries beyond it. Once that is gone, there is only the prestige—and no doubt that is very great—which is left to it as an important world port. I am far from denying that that is a very important matter. The Government will approach the question of the future rule of Constantinople with an absolutely open mind, while I think that those considerations must be borne in mind in dealing with that question.

There was one other suggestion made about the future government of Armenia. My hon. Friend the Member for Donegal (Mr. Law) said that he hoped that the League of Nations would be utilised as an instrument for the government of Armenia. In that matter I speak for myself, as I have already said in public and I do not mind saying it again, I think most emphatically that is one of the matters which we should control, and which ought to be properly entrusted to the League of Nations in some form or another. That especially, I think, should be the fact, but I cannot pretend whilst speaking on that matter

to be the spokesman of the Government. I am expressing my own opinions.

Colonel WEDGWOOD: Would you include Lesser Armenia?

Lord R. CECIL: I was merely speaking in general terms. As to the extent of the new government of Armenia, whatever it may be, I will say a word. Very little was said in the course of the Debate about the boundaries of the new State of Armenia. I recognise fully the strength of the observations that we must not allow the misdeeds of the Turks to diminish the patrimony of the Armenians. That is the general principle. I recognise the great force of what the hon. Member said—that there ought to be no division of Armenia, and that it ought to be treated as one whole. Having said all that, do not think I ought to go further and attempt to draw on the map the boundary which would be the result of the application of these principles. All that I will say is this: My hon. Friend the Member for Donegal asked me whether the Government, in saying that they would free Armenia from the misrule of the Turks, had some reservation in their minds, meaning that they would allow the rule to continue, but not the misrule. As far as I am concerned—and I believe in this matter I am speaking for the Government—I should be deeply disappointed if any shred or shadow of Turkish government were left in Armenia.

Mr. H. LAW: Wherever the Turks ruled.

Lord R. CECIL: There are certain scattered populations, scattered about really Turkish country, for which it may be impossible to provide separate government, but, speaking broadly, our object is the liberation of all those populations. It is not only the Armenians, it is the Kurds, the Arabs, the Jew, the Greeks—all of them are entitled to our assistance. As far as Armenia is concerned, I have given my views in very unmistakable terms. With regard to the Arabs, I may say exactly the same thing. As to the Kurds, I hope for the same result. As far as the Greeks are concerned, undoubtedly they are entitled to our protection, but, as the hon. Gentleman knows, the problem is a difficult one. They are spread all along the coast, and I think they ought to enjoy protection.

Mr. LAW: The purpose and intention will be the same?

Lord R. CECIL: The purpose and intention will be the same.

Colonel WEDGWOOD: Do you mean by that that they will not be under the Turkish flag?

Lord R. CECIL: Certainly I do, as far as Armenia is concerned. Of course that is only as regards the British Government. I personally think that necessary, because I share to the full the view which has been expressed that the enemy in this matter is the Turkish Government. I believe it to be true— and the evidence as far as I have ever examined it bears it out—that everyone of the atrocities in Armenia has not been the result of casual ferocity of isolated Turkish brigands, but has been ordered from Constantinople in every case, as far as I know. That is the central fact one must realise in dealing with the situation. The Turkish policy throughout has been to create disorder, and then to suppress it. It is not a religious question. The Arabs, for instance, have always protected the Armenians; and when we came to Aleppo, we found several bodies of Armenians living there under the protection of the Arabs. In the same way, I believe there is no reason why the Kurds and Armenians should not live perfectly well together, if once the Turkish influence were removed. There are signs already that the Kurds and the Armenians are prepared to make terms with one another, and to arrange to live together. But the feature of the Turkish policy was to stir up every division in the subject races, in order to make them less powerful, and also in order to justify any atrocity they chose to carry out at any time. Therefore I agree most fully that the Turkish Government has proved itself absolutely incapable of ruling any subject races, that its days are now, I trust, at an end, and I hope will never be allowed to begin again.

There are symptoms that even now the Turks have not learned their lesson—that they are showing signs of carrying on their old policy of delay, of raising with incredible fertility every kind of objection to any course which is likely to produce lasting improvement; and, if they had the opportunity, no doubt they would try every device of setting one Western European nation against another. But I venture to say this—and say it with all feeling of responsibility that those days are ended, and that the Turks will make a profound mistake if they do not realise that their power of delay and resistance to reform is finally finished. They are now absolutely in our power; and the only way that they can hope to receive clemency or consideration will be if they show that they have really mended their ways, and hasten to carry out the terms of the Armistice to which they have agreed, as well as the other conditions which will be put upon them by the justice of the conquerors, without any hesitation, and without any effort to avoid doing that which will certainly be forced upon them.

[Debate continues on other issues]

APPENDIXES

APPENDIXES

Appendix I

The following declaration was initiated by the Russian Government in April 1915.* *Invoking the precedent of an earlier European intervention in Lebanon in 1860, following the massacre of Christians there, the Russians suggested similar joint action against Ottoman Turkish leaders for reported atrocities against Armenians.† The British Government was reluctant to support such a declaration because of a lack of information, and because Great Britain had already threatened action against Ottoman leaders following the use of Allied nationals as human shields at Gallipoli.‡ It was the opinion of the Foreign Office that too many such threats would undermine their effectiveness.** Nevertheless, the British Government decided to support the Russian initiative as a political necessity to placate the Russian Government and Armenians serving in Russian armies.†† Russian-Armenians were particularly aware of the massacres reported in Ottoman Turkey, because many survivors fled to safety behind Russian lines. Although the British Government did not have an active interest in Armenians at this time—the absolute priority was defeating the Germans in Europe and winning the war—the Foreign Office got involved with the Armenian issue because of Russian pressure.*

Some authors have argued that the May declaration signified a critical understanding of the Armenian Genocide by the British Government, and that the term "crimes against humanity," which was used in the declaration, had a profound legal significance. However, the actual evidence suggests that the British Government did not know of the

---

* See FO 371/2488/51010. For a copy of the proposed Russian text, see FO371/2488/58387.

† FO 371/2488/51010. For the earlier precedent, see Duke of Argyll, *Our Responsibilities for Turkey: Facts and Memories of Forty Years*, (London: John Murray, 1896, pp. 40-42), (London: Sterndale Classics, 2003, pp.22-23).

‡ See chapter ix in Henry Morgenthau, *Ambassador Morgenthau's Story*, (Princeton and London: Gomidas Institute, 2000), (London: Sterndale Classics, 2003).

** See FO371/2488/59097.

†† Regarding the proposed diplomatic note of the Russian government, Sir E. Grey commented, "...it seems to me that we do not possess sufficently trustworthy data on which to base such a message..." Sir E. Grey to Sir F. Bertie (British Embassy, Petrograd), 2 May 1915. FO371/2488/57956. Furthermore, Sir Edward Grey questioned the wisdom of such a note: "It seems to me that such a pronouncement will have no moderating effect whatever on the Turkish authorities and indeed might, on the contrary, instigate it to be still more vindictive towards Christians. We shall, when the occasion arrives, be equally free to take what measures we consider justifiable and necessary against the guilty Turkish authorities, whether we had or had not previously issued a public notification of our intentions...." Sir E. Grey to Sir F. Bertie, 12 May 1915, FO371/2488/58387.

reported atrocities in Armenia at that time, and the British version of the declaration did not actually use the phrase "crimes against humanity." While the French and Russian Governments used the latter expression, they used it as a matter of word-play on the original Russian draft, which charged Ottoman leaders with "crimes against Christianity and civilization." British understanding of the Armenian Genocide did not materialise until much later, after the mass deportations and massacres of the summer of 1915, and the dissemination of critical evidence through the United States (See Appendix II).

[From Foreign Office press office for publication in Monday morning papers (23 May 1915)]*

H.M. Government, in common with the Governments of France and Russia, make the following public declaration:-

For about the last month Kurds and the Turkish population of Armenia have been engaged in massacring Armenians with connivance and often help of Ottoman Authorities. Such massacres took place about the middle of April, at Erzroum, Dertchan, Egin, Bitlis, Sassoun, Moush, Zeitun, and in all Cilicia.

Inhabitants of about 100 villages near Van were all assassinated. In town itself Armenians' quarter is besieged by Kurds. At the same time Ottoman Government at Constantinople is raging against inoffensive Armenian population.

In face of these fresh crimes committed by Turkey the Allied Governments announce publicly to the Sublime Porte that they will hold all the members of the Ottoman Government, as well as such of their agents as are implicated, personally responsible for Armenian massacres."†

---

* PRO, FO371/2488/63095.

† The original draft from the Russians was phrased "...crimes committed by Turkey against Christianity and civilisation..." See FO371/2488/58387. The British and French governments found this wording objectionable due to the possible sensibilities of their Muslim subjects. While the British dropped the phrase "against Christianity and civilisation", the Russian and French versions replaced it with "...crimes committed by Turkey against humanity and civilisation" See FO371/2488/65759.

Appendix II

The October 4th 1915 press release of the Committee on Armenian Atrocities (New York) was possibly the singlemost important document to influence British Parliamentary discussions of the Armenian Genocide, and it led the way to a formal Parliamentary investigation into the reported atrocities against Armenians. Until the October 4th press release, British understanding of these atrocities was hampered by a lack of reliable information due to Ottoman censorship and misinformation campaigns.

Although the British Government severed its relations with Ottoman Turkey when the latter entered WWI alongside the Central Powers, the United States maintained its neutrality and retained its ties with Turkey until April 1917. Consequently, the State Department was well informed of events in the Ottoman Empire by its representatives and tried to ameliorate the condition of Armenians. It was the continuing persecution of Armenians which led to direct American action by the end of the year (while the United States was still a neutral power). In September 1915, the State Department began leaking sensitive information on the plight of Armenians in an effort to publicise the issue, raise funds, and provide relief where possible. The United States became the most important source of information on the Armenian Genocide for British authorities. Over half of all reports in the 1916 British Parliamentary report on the Armenian Genocide came from the United States. These reports included despatches filed by US Consuls in the interior of Turkey, as well as reports from Henry Morgenthau, the US Ambassador to Constantinople. The authority and substance of these reports left little to dispute— "...a campaign of race extermination is in progress" (Henry Morgenthau, 16 July 1915) "...it is nothing less than the extermination of the Armenian race" (J.B. Jackson, US Consul at Aleppo, 3 August 1915) "...the general plan to dispose of the Armenian race" (Leslie Davis, US Consul at Harpoot, 10 August 1915).

The October 4th press release provided the substance of James Bryce's seminal speech at the House of Lords two days later, as well as Aneurin Williams' speech in the House of Commons on 16 November. Bryce declared his hand to Lord Cromer when he wrote on the eve of his seminal speech: "You will be sorry to hear that the accounts which have reached the U.S. Government from its Embassy in Constantinople and the American Mission Board from its missionaries describe the cruelties and deportations practised by the Turks in Armenia as even more horrible than we had gathered from such news as had previously found its way out of the country. Much of these accounts has now been published in a Report prepared by the American Committee which is now reaching this country and a copy of which I will try to get for you. Of course it cannot disclose the *sources of the information, but I have been told privately whence it comes, and there can be no doubt as to its substantial accuracy. One shocking report comes from a German missionary.* "*

The October speech at the House of Lords proved to be a turning point in the development of the British government's understanding of the Armenian Genocide. Until the appearance of this report, British authorities, despite their sympathies for Armenians, remained reticent to pursue the Armenian issue. The matter was rife with political pitfalls, especially as "Muslim opinion" could be inflamed in the British Empire with a weak case against the Ottoman Turks. The October 4th press release presented sufficient evidence to allow a shift in policy, and it led to the 1916 Parliamentary Blue Book on the Armenian Genocide.

Editorial Policy

The Report of the Committee on Armenian Atrocities which follows this introduction appears in its entirety and includes some key annotations, including references to original archival copies of reports wherever they could be traced.† Appearing in brackets is information that was withheld in the October 4 press release to safeguard sources. Such information appears in brackets. All other annotations appear as footnotes. The reports have been numbered I-XXV, skipping numbers XIII and XX, as in the original October 4 press release.

Ara Sarafian
November 2002

---

* *Bryce to Lord Cromer communication dated 5 October 1915, PRO, FO 633/24/204. James Bryce's October 6th speech was included (with corrections) into a pamphlet published soon afterwards. See Arnold Toynbee,* Armenian Atrocities: The Murder of a Nation, *London, New York, Toronto: Hodder and Stoughton, 1915.*

† *This document has been annotated using the following key sources: 1. The State Department archives, Record Group 59 on the Internal Affairs of Turkey, 1910-1929, National Archives, Washington D.C. (microfilm collection); 2. Arnold Toynbee and James Bryce,* The Treatment of the Armenians in the Ottoman Empire, 1915-16: Documents Presented to Viscount Grey of Falloden by Viscount Bryce (London 1916), *and,* Key to Names of Persons and Places Withheld from Publication in the Original Edition of "The Treatment of the Armenians in the Ottoman Empire, 1915-16: Documents Presented to Viscount Grey of Falloden by Viscount Bryce" *([London 1916], Miscellaneous no 31); 3. Barton to Toynbee communication dated March 6 1915, Toynbee Papers, FO. 96, file 205, p. 141-143.*

Release for Publication in Papers of Monday, Oct. 4, 1915

A committee, consisting of Charles R. Crane, Samuel T. Dutton, Cleveland H. Dodge, Arthur C. James, Stephen S. Wise, Frank Mason North, John R. Mott, Stanley White, H. G. Benneyan, James L. Barton, William Sloane, William L. Haven, George A. Plimpton, Karl Davis Robinson, Frederick Lynch, Norman Hopgood, and others representing American interests in the Turkish Empire, have made careful and extensive investigation of the evidence bearing upon the atrocities inflicted upon Armenians in Turkey, and have collected a mass of statements upon the subject from sources that are unquestioned as to the veracity, integrity and authority of the writers. For reasons that will be obvious to all, the names and position of the various writers cannot be given at this time. These are known to the committee, who vouch for them and for their statements. In most cases it will be necessary to conceal the place from which the statements were written, and even the name of the cities and towns referred to, in order that the writer or his interests may not suffer irreparable harm.

We quote here from a few of these documents which are in the possession of the committee:

I[*]

April 27. "Movement against Armenians forms part of a concerted movement against all non-Turkish and mission [*sic*, union] and progress element, including Zionists." Unfavorable reports received about Armenians in the interior provinces.

II[†]

April 30. Continued reports of persecution, plunder and massacre of Armenians in the interior parts of the country. Treatment of the Armenians of Zeitoun and Marash with incredible severity. Scattering a large number of the innocent population a part of a campaign.

III[‡]

July 10. Persecution of Armenians assuming unprecedented proportions. Reports from widely scattered regions indicate systematic attempt to uproot peaceful Armenian populations, and through arbitrary arrests, terrible tortures, wholesale

---

[*] Confidential cable despatch, Ambassador Morgenthau to Secretary of State, dated April 27 1915. National Archives (Washington DC), RG 59, 867.4016/58.

[†] Confidential cable despatch, Ambassador Morgenthau to Secretary of State, dated April 30 1915. National Archives (Washington DC), RG 59, 867.4016/59.

[‡] Confidential cable despatch, Ambassador Morgenthau to Secretary of State, dated July 10 1915. National Archives (Washington DC), RG 59, 867.4016/74.

expulsions and deportations from one end of the empire to the other accompanied by frequent instances of rape, pillage and murder, turning into massacre, to bring destitution and destruction upon them. This is not in response to fanatical or popular demand, but is purely arbitrary, and directed from Constantinople.

Untold misery, disease, starvation and loss of life will go on unchecked.

IV*

July 13. "I am informed that the Turkish authorities have, since May 1st, deported over 40,000 Ottoman Greeks from the islands and the coast of Marmora to interior Turkish Moslem villages, and that they are filling the Greek villages with refugees from Macedonia."

V†

July 16. "Deportation of and excesses against peaceful Armenians is increasing, and from harrowing reports of eye-witnesses it appears that a campaign of race extermination is in progress." Protests and threats are unavailing and probably incite the Ottoman government to more drastic measures, as they are determined to disclaim responsibility for their absolute disregard of capitulations, and I believe nothing short of actual force, which obviously the United States is not in a position to exert, would adequately meet the situation.

VI‡

July 31. "Armenians, mostly women and children, deported from the Erzroom district, have been massacred near Kemakh, between Erzroom and Harpoot." Similar reports from other sources, that probably few of these refugees will reach their destination.

---

* Cable despatch, Ambassador Morgenthau to Secretary of State, dated July 13 1915. National Archives (Washington DC), RG 59, 867.4016/75.

† Confidential cable despatch, Ambassador Morgenthau to Secretary of State, dated July 16 1915. National Archives (Washington DC), RG 59, 867.4016/76.

‡ Cable despatch, Ambassador Morgenthau to Secretary of State, dated July 31, 1915. National Archives (Washington DC), RG 59, 867.4016/83.

VII[*]

The deportation began some six weeks ago with 180 families from Zeitoun; since which time all the inhabitants of that place and its neighboring villages have been deported; also most of the Christians in Albustan, many from Hadjin, Sis, Kars Pazar, Hassan Beyli and Deort Yol.

The numbers involved are approximately, to date, 26,500. Of these, about 5,000 have been sent to the Konieh region, 5,500 are in Aleppo and surrounding towns and villages, and the remainder are in Der Zor, Racca, and various places in Mesopotamia, even as far as the neighborhood of Bagdad.

The process is still going on, and there is no telling how far it may [be] carried. The orders already issued will bring the number in this region up to 32,000, and there have been as yet none exiled from Aintab, and very few from Marash and Oorfa The following is the text of the government order covering the case. Art. 2nd.: "The commanders of the army, of independent army corps and of divisions may, in case of military necessity, and in case they suspect espionage or treason, send away, either or in mass, the inhabitants of villages or town, and install them in other places."

The orders of commanders may have been reasonably humane; but the execution of them has been for the most part unnecessarily harsh, and in many cases accompanied by horrible brutality to women and children, to the sick and the aged. Whole villages were deported at an hour's notice, with no opportunity to prepare for the journey, not even, in some cases, to gather together the scattered members of the family, so that little children were left behind. At the mountain village of Geben the women were at the washtub, and were compelled to leave their wet clothes in the water and take the road barefooted and half clad just as they were. In some cases they were able to carry part of their scanty household furniture, or implements of agriculture, but for the most part they were neither to carry anything, nor to sell it, even where there was time to do so.

In Hadjin, well-to-do people, who had prepared food and bedding for the road were obliged to leave it in the street, and afterward suffered greatly from hunger.

In many cases the men were (those of military age were nearly all in the army) bound tightly together with ropes or chains. Women with little children in their arms, or in the last days of pregnancy, were driven along under the whip like cattle. Three different cases came under my knowledge where the woman was delivered on the road, and because her brutal driver hurried her along she died of hemorrhage. I also know of one case where the gendarme in charge was a humane man, and allowed the poor woman several hours rest, and then procured a wagon for her to ride in. Some

[*] Letter from Dr. Shepard of Aintab, dated June 20, 1915. See *The Treatment of Armenians in the Ottoman Empire,* Report No 120.

women became so completely worn out and hopeless that they left their infants beside the road. Many women and girls have been outraged. At one place the commander of gendarmerie openly told the men to whom he consigned a large company that they were at liberty to do what they chose with the women and girls.

As to subsistence, there has been a great difference in different places. In some places the government has fed them, in some places it has permitted the inhabitants to feed them. In some places it has neither fed them or permitted others to do so. There has been much hunger, thirst and sickness, and some real starvation and death.

These people are being scattered in small units, three or four families in a place, among a population of different race and religion, and speaking a different language. I speak of them as being composed of families, but four-fifths of them are women and children, and what men there are are for the most part old or incompetent.

If a means is not found to aid them through the next few months, until they get established in their new surroundings, two-thirds or three-fourths of them will die of starvation and disease.

VIII*

I was called to a house one day where I saw a sheet which originated from the prison and which was being sent to the wash. This sheet was covered with blood and running in long streams. I was also shown clothes which were drenched and exceedingly dirty. It was a puzzle to me what they could possibly have done to the prisoners but I got to the bottom of the matter by the help of two very reliable persons who witnessed part of it themselves.

The prisoner is put in a room (similar to the times of the Romans). Gendarmes standing in twos at both sides and two at the end of the room administer each in their turn bastinadoes as long as they have enough force in them. At the times of the Romans, forty strokes were administered at the very most; in this place however 200, 300, 500, even 800 strokes are administered. The foot swells up, then bursts open, due to the numerous blows, and thus the blood spurts out. The prisoner is then carried back into prison and brought to bed by the rest of the prisoners - this explains the bloody sheet. The prisoners who become unconscious after these blows are revived through the means of some cold water which is thrown on their heads and which accounts for the wet and dirty clothes. On the next day, or more exactly, during the night, as all ill-treatments are carried on at night in [Cesarea], as well as in [Everek], the whole bastinadoing is being carried on again in spite of swollen feet and their wounds. I was then in [Zingidere], but in that prison there were also thirty

---

* Copy of report by Fr. W.H. Hunecke (n/d) forwarded Ambassador Morgenthau to Secretary of State, dated July 20 1915. National Archives (Washington DC), RG 59, 867.4016/94.

prisoners in number, and all had their feet in such a state that they begun to burn and had to be amputated, or were already taken off. These have been ill-treated to this extent in [Everek], and also by the cruel Mutessarif in [Cesarea]. A young man was beaten to death within the space of five minutes. Apart from the bastonadoing, other methods were employed, too, such as putting hot irons on the chest. A forger, who was suspected to have forged the shells of the bombs, was let free only after his toes were burned off with sulphur (called Kerab). I have seen the wounds. Four weeks ago we received news that the Caimakam of [Everek] had had ten to eighteen people shot in a district between [Everek] and [Indeschesu]. Shortly after this had happened an order was promulgated which concerned the Christians of [Indeschesu], and which demanded that they all leave the place within three-quarters of an hour. Among these were several women who gave birth to children on the way, and which they in their desperation, threw into the water. Many men were recalled, and it is impossible to say how many were secretly murdered and how many will still be butchered. I wish to state that the inhabitants of [Indeschesu] are so terribly ignorant that I really never saw the like, and I therefore feel convinced that not one single person had ever dreamt of opposing the authorities. Neither from the Turks nor from the Christians have I ever heard that one of these people had in the four months described above ever rebelled, and it is the Caimakam alone who says so in order to excuse his deeds. And yet the Caimakam always declares: "No one dares oppose me." When I ventured to protest to the Caimakam in all kindness against the bloody sheets, he replied as follows: "If the law and the Sultan were to forbid it, I would in spite of it all, carry these things out and do as I please." Three weeks ago in [Everek], when I was engaged in getting ready to go off, I noticed two gendarmes riding in the direction of the mountains with an inhabitant of [Indeschesu] who had been expelled and then recalled. They (gendarmes) returned without the man and gave as excuse that the man escaped, which is of course out of the question, the man's feet being completely swollen, and while he rode an ass and the gendarmes were on horseback. The German consul of Aleppo estimates the number of deported to be 30,000. Five thousand people were deported to the unhealthy spot of Sultani, in the district of Konia. The government gave in the first days some bread. When the bread was finished and they received none, the misery was heartrending. According to Mr [Dodd], [Konia], the rich were also deported to Sultani, who shared their bread with the poor as long as their money lasted, which was not very long, of course. Mr [Dodd] begged the Vali for permission to supply the people with breaid but he replied that the government attends to this, and the people did not want any.

IX[*]

The trouble for the Armenians began, as for all other nationalities, with the collection of soldiers. The government swept all men possible for military service. Hundreds of the breadwinners marched away, leaving their wives and children without means of support. In many cases the last bit of money was given to fit out the departing soldier, leaving the family in a pitifully destitute condition. A number of Armenians were quite well off and paid their military exemption fee. A much larger number escaped in one way and another, so there were more Armenians than Turks left in the city after the soldiers had gone. This made the government suspicious and fearful. The discovery of Armenian plots against the government in other places added to this feeling. The special Armenian troubles began in the beginning of May. In the middle of the night about twenty of the leading men of the national Armenian political parties were gathered up and sent to where they have been imprisoned ever since. In June the government began looking for weapons. Some of the Armenians were seized, and, by torture, the confession was extracted that a large number of arms were in the hands of different Armenians. A second inquisition began. The bastinado was used frequently, as well as fire torture (in some cases eyes are said to have been put out). Many guns were delivered, but not all. The people were afraid that if they gave up their arms, they would be massacred as in 1895. Arms had been brought in after the declaration of the constitution with the permission of the government, and were for self-defense only. The torture continued, and under its influence one fact after another leaked out. Under the nervous strain and physical suffering many things were said which had no foundation in fact. Those inflicting the torture would tell the victim what they expected him to confess, and then beat him until he did it. The college mechanic had constructed an iron shot for the athletic games, and was beaten terribly in all effort to fasten the making of bombs on the college. Some bombs were discovered in the Armenian cemetery, which aroused the fury of the Turks to white heat. It should be said that it is very probable that these bombs had been buried there in the days of Abdul Hamid.

On Saturday, June 26, about 1 p. m., the gendarmes went through the town gathering up all the Armenian men they could find - old and young, rich and poor, sick and well. In some cases houses were broken into, and sick men dragged from their beds. They were imprisoned in the barracks, and during the next few days were sent off toward [Sivas] in groups of from thirty to one hundred and fifty. They were sent on foot, and many were robbed of shoes and other articles of clothing. Some were in chains. The first group reached [Sivas] and sent word from various places. (It is said that this was a scheme of the government in order to encourage the rest. None of the rest have been heard from. Various reports have been circulated, the only one generally accepted being that they were killed. One Greek driver reported seeing the mound under which they were buried. Another man in touch with the government, in answer to a direct question, admitted that the men had been killed.)

---

[*] Report of American teacher of Marsovan College (n/d), forwarded Ambassador Morgenthau to Secretary of State, dated July 26 1915. National Archives (Washington DC), RG 59, 867.4016/ 106. See *The Treatment of Armenians in the Ottoman Empire*, Report No 86.

Through the intervention of a Turk the college was able to free those of its teachers already taken, and obtain a stay of proceedings against all of its teachers and employees, by the payment of the sum of 275 Turkish liras. Later this same Turk said that he believed that he could obtain the permanent exemption of the entire college group by the payment of a further sum of 300 liras. The money was promised, but after some negotiations, which showed that no definite assurance of exemption would be forthcoming, the matter was dropped.

Following the sending of the groups of Armenians in the direction of [Sivas], criers went through the streets of the town announcing that all male Armenians between the ages of fifteen and seventy were to report at the barracks. The announcement further stated that their refusal to obey would result in their being killed and their houses being burned. The Armenian priests went from house to house, advising the people to obey this announcement. Those reporting at the barracks were sent away in groups, the result being that within a few days practically all of the Armenian men were removed from the city.

On the third or fourth of July the order was issued that the women and children should be ready to leave on the following Wednesday. The people were informed that one ox cart was to be provided by the government for each house, and that they could carry only one day's food supply, a few piastres, and a small bundle of clothing. The people made preparation for carrying out these orders by selling whatever household possessions they could in the street. Articles were sold at less than 10 per cent of their usual value, and Turks from the neighboring villages filled the streets, hunting for bargains. In some places these Turks took articles by force, but the government punished all such cases when detected.

On July 5, before the order for the expulsion of the women was carried out, [Dr Marden] went to the government to protest against the execution of this order in the name of humanity. He was told that this order did not originate with the local officials, but that the orders had come from those higher up not to leave a single Armenian in the city. The commandant, however, promised to leave the college to the last, and gave permission for all people connected with the American institutions to move into the college compound. This they did, and at one time over 300 Armenians were living on the college premises.

The population had been ordered to be ready to depart Wednesday. But on Tuesday, about 3:30 a.m., the ox carts appeared at the doors of the first district to be removed, and the people were ordered to depart at once. Some were dragged from their beds without even sufficient clothing. All the morning the ox carts creaked out of the town, laden with women and children, and here and there a man who had escaped the previous deportations. The women and girls all wore the Turkish costume, that their faces might not be exposed to the gaze of drivers and gendarmes - a brutal lot of men brought in from other regions. In many cases the husbands and brothers of these same women were away in the army, fighting for the Turkish government.

The panic in the city was terrible. The people felt that the government was determined to exterminate the Armenian race, and they were powerless to resist. The people were sure that the men were being killed and the women kidnapped. Many of the convicts in the prison had been released, and the mountains around [Marsovan] were full of bands of outlaws. It was feared that the women and children were taken some distance from the city and left to the mercy of these men. However that may be, there are provable cases of the kidnapping of attractive young girls by the Turkish officials of [Marsovan]. One Moslem reported that a gendarme had offered to sell him two girls for a mejidieh. The women believed that they were going to worse than death and many carried poison in their pockets to use if necessary. Some carried picks and shovels to bury those they knew would die by the wayside. During this reign of terror notice was given that escape was easy; that any one who accepted Islam would be allowed to remain safely at home. The offices of the lawyers who recorded applications were crowded with people petitioning to become Mohammedans. Many did it for the sake of their women and children, feeling that it would be a matter of only a few weeks before relief could come.

This deportation continued at intervals for about two weeks. It is estimated that out of about 12,000 Armenians in [Marsovan] only a few hundred were left. Even those who offered to accept Islam were sent away. At the time of writing, no definite word has been heard from any of these groups. (One Greek driver reported that at a little village a few hours from Marsovan, the few men were separated from the women, were beaten and chained, and sent on in a separate group. A Turkish driver reported seeing the caravan two days' journey from [Marsovan]. The people were so covered with dust that features were scarcely distinguishable.) Even if the lives of these exiles are being protected, it is a question how many will be able to endure the hardships of the journey over the hot, dusty hills, with no protection from the sun, with poor food and little water, and the ever-present fear of death, or some worse fate.

Most of the Armenians in the [Marsovan] district were absolutely hopeless. Many said that it was worse than a massacre. No one knew what was coming, but all felt that it was the end. Even the pastors and leaders could offer no word of encouragement or hope. Many began to doubt even the existence of God. Under the severe strain many individuals became demented, some of them permanently. There were also some examples of the greatest heroism and faith, and some started out on the journey courageously and calmly, saying in farewell.. "Pray for us. We will not see you again in this world, but sometime we will meet again."

X[*]

I have the honor to inform you that two days ago an order was received here for the immediate deportation of the entire Armenian population of [Mersina], consisting of about 1,800 souls. Yesterday nearly 300 persons were sent to [Adana] and to-day many more have been ordered to be ready to leave. In anticipation of their deportation, the Armenians are selling all their non-portable goods for a song. Sewing machines sold for 1.5 medjidies, iron bedsteads for a few piastres, etc. The government is allowing each person only a few metallics per day for food, and transports only a little baggage. The present destination of the deported persons is [Adana]. Apart from their actual distress and misery, the terror of these people is indescribable. Stories of the massacre of thousands of Armenians in the interior now reach here. Some of these appear to be well founded, but I presume the [Embassy] has been fully informed of what has transpired in the regions of [Cesarea, Sivas and Diarbekir, not to mention Van].

XI[†]

The children attending the American school conducted by [Dr and Mrs Crawford], also those children left with them by persons being deported, have all been taken and placed in a school organized by a local committee, of which the [Vali] is president, and the Greek metropolitan vice-president. Into this school all the Armenian children, females up to fifteen years and males to ten years of age, are being placed as soon as the parents are sent off. Children above these ages go with their parents.

XII[‡]

On Saturday, June 26, the proclamation regarding the deportation of all Armenians was posted in the streets. On Thursday, July 1, all the streets were guarded by gendarmes with fixed bayonets, and the work of driving the Armenians from their homes began. Groups of men, women and children with loads and bundles on their backs, were collected in a short cross street near the consulate, and when a hundred or so had been gathered, they were driven past the consulate on the road toward

---

[*] Copy of consular report from Mersine, Edward I. Nathan to Ambassador Morgenthau, dated August 7 1915, forwarded Ambassador Morgenthau to the Secretary of State on Aug. 15, 1915. National Archives (Washington DC), RG 59, 867.4016/124. See *The Treatment of Armenians in the Ottoman Empire,* Report No 115.

[†] Consular report from Trebizond, Oscar S. Heizer to Ambassador Morgenthau, dated July 3 1915, forwarded Ambassador Morgenthau to the Secretary of State on July 15 1915. National Archives (Washington DC), RG 59, 867.4016/94.

[‡] Consular report from Trebizond, Oscar S. Heizer to Secretary of State, dated July 29 1915. National Archives (Washington DC), RG 59, 867.4016/128. See *The Treatment of Armenians in the Ottoman Empire,* Toynbee/Bryce, Report No 72.

[Gumushhané and Erzingan] in the heat and dust by gendarmes with fixed bayonets. They were held outside the city until a group of about 2,000 were collected, then sent on. Three such groups, making about 6,000, were sent from here during the first three days, and smaller groups from [Trebizond] and the vicinity sent later amounted to about 4,000 more. The weeping and wailing of the women and children was most heartrending. Some of these people were from wealthy and refined circles. Some were accustomed to luxury and ease. There were clergymen, merchants, bankers, lawyers, mechanics, tailors and men from every walk of life. The governor-general told me they were allowed to make arrangements for carriages, but nobody seemed to be making any arrangements. I know of one wealthy merchant, however, who paid Lt. 15 ($66.00) for a carriage to take himself and wife to [Djevizlik], and when he arrived at the station where they were being collected, at [Deyermendéré], about ten minutes from the city, they were commanded by the gendarmes to leave the carriage which was sent back to the city. The whole Mohammedan population knew these people were to be their prey from the beginning, and they were treated as criminals. In the first place, from the date of the proclamation, June 25, no Armenian was allowed to sell anything, and everybody was forbidden, wider penalty, to buy anything from them. How then, were they to provide funds for the journey? For six or eight months there has been no business whatever in [Trebizond], and people have been eating up their capital. Why should they have been prohibited from selling rugs or anything they had to sell to secure needed money for the journey? Many persons who had goods which they could have sold if they had been allowed to do so were obliged to start off on foot without funds and with what they could gather up from their homes and carry on their backs. Such persons naturally soon became so weak that they fell behind and were bayoneted and thrown into the river, and their bodies floated down past [Trebizond] to the sea, or lodged in the shallow river on rocks, where they remained for ten or twelve days and putrified to the disgust of travelers who were obliged to pass that way. I have talked with eye-witnesses, who state there were many naked bodies to be seen on snags in the river fifteen days after the affair occurred, and that the smell was something terrible.

On the 17th of July, while out horseback riding with the German [Consul], we came across three Turks digging a grave in the sand for a naked body which we saw in the river nearby. The corpse looked as though it had been in the water for ten days or more. The Turks said they had just buried four more further up the river. Another Turk told us that a body had floated down the river and out into the sea a few moments before we arrived.

By July 6 (Tuesday), all the Armenian houses in [Trebizond], about 1,000, had been emptied of inhabitants and the people sent off. There was no inquiry as to who were guilty or who were innocent of any movement against the government. If a person was an Armenian that was sufficient reason for being treated as a criminal and deported. At first all were to go except the sick who were taken to the municipal hospital until they were well enough to go. Later an exception was made for old men and women, pregnant women, children, those in government employ and Catholic Armenians. Finally it was decided that the old men and women and the Catholics must go and they were sent along towards the last. A number of lighters have been loaded with people at different times and sent off towards [Samsoun]. It is generally believed that such persons were drowned. During the early days before the deportation commenced, a large caique or lighter was loaded with men supposed to be members of the Armenian committee, and sent off towards [Samsoun]. Two days later a certain Russian subject, and one of those who left in the boat, returned overland to [Trebizond], badly wounded about the head and so crazy he could not make himself understood. All he could say was "Boom, boom." He was arrested by the authorities and taken to the municipal hospital, where he died the following day. A Turk said this boat was met not far from [Trebizond] by another boat containing gendarmes, who proceeded to kill all the men and throw them overboard. They thought they had killed them all, but this Russian, who was big and powerful, was only wounded and swam ashore unnoticed. A number of such caiques have left loaded with men and usually they return empty after a few hours.

[Tots], a village about two hours from [Trebizond], is inhabited by Gregorian and Catholic Armenians and Turks. A wealthy and influential Armenian, together with his two sons, according to a reliable witness, were placed one behind the other and shot through. Forty-five men and women were taken a short distance from the village into a valley. The women were first outraged by the officers of the gendarmerie, and then turned over to the gendarmes to dispose of. According to this witness a child was killed by beating its brains out on a rock. The men were all killed, and not a single person survived from this group of forty-five.

The plan to save the children by placing them in schools or orphanages in [Trebizond], under the care of a committee organized and supported by the Greek Archbishop, of which the Vali was president and the Archbishop vice-president, with three Mohammedan and three Christian members, has been abandoned, and the girls are now being given exclusively to Mohammedan families and thus scattered. The suppression of the orphanages and the scattering of the children was a great disappointment to this [Consulate] and to the Greek Archbishop who had worked hard for the plan and secured the support of the Vali, but the head of the Committee of Union and Progress, who was opposed to the plan, succeeded in thwarting it very quickly. Many of the boys appear to have been sent to [Platana] to be distributed among the farmers. The best looking of the older girls, who were retained as caretakers in these orphanages, are kept in houses for the pleasure of members of the gang which seems to rule affairs here. I hear on good authority that a member of the Committee of Union and Progress here has ten of the handsomest girls in a house in the central part of the city for the use of himself and friends. Some of the small girls have been taken into respectable Mohammedan houses. Several of the former pupils of the American Mission are now in Mohammedan homes near the Mission, and have not been visited by [Mrs. Crawford], but of course the majority of them are not so fortunate.

The 1,000 Armenian houses are being emptied of furniture by the police one after the other. The furniture, bedding and everything of value is being stored in large buildings about the city. There is no attempt at classification, and the idea of keeping the property in "bales under the protection of the government to be returned to the owners on their return" is simply ridiculous. The goods are piled in without any attempt at labeling or systematic storage. A crowd of Turkish women and children follow the police about like a lot of vultures, and seize anything they can lay their hands on, and when the more valuable things are carried out of a house by the police they rush in and take the balance. I see this performance every day with my own eyes. I suppose it will take several weeks to empty all the houses, and then the Armenian shops and stores will be cleared out. The commission which has this matter in hand is now talking of selling this great collection of household goods and properties in order to pay the debts of the Armenians. The German Consul told me that he did not believe the Armenians would be permitted to return to [Trebizond], even after the end of the war.

I have just been talking with a young man who has been performing his military service on the "inshaat tabouri" (construction regiment), working on the roads out toward Gumushhane. He told me that 15 days ago all the Armenians, about 180, were separated from the other workmen and marched off some distance from the camp and shot. He heard the report of the rifles and later was one of the number sent to bury the bodies, which he stated were all naked, having been stripped of clothing.

A number of bodies of women and children have lately been thrown up by the sea upon the sandy beach below the walls of the Italian Monastery here in [Trebizond], and were buried by Greek women in the sand where they were found.

XIV[*]

June 28, 1915. I wish to inform you of conditions here. They are very bad and daily getting worse. I suppose [the Maynards] told you of the horrible things taking place in [Diarbekir]. Just such a reign of terror has begun in this city also. Daily the police are searching the houses of the Armenians for weapons, and not finding any, they are

---

[*] Copy of Consular report from Aleppo (quoting letter from Mr. Leslie in Ourfa), J.B. Jackson to Ambassador Morgenthau, dated June 28 1915, forwarded Ambassador Morgenthau to Secretary of State, dated July 13 1915. National Archives, RG 59, 867.4016/92. See *The Treatment of Armenians in the Ottoman Empire,* Toynbee/Bryce, Report No. 133.

taking the best and most honorable men and imprisoning them; some of them they are exiling, and others they are torturing with red hot irons to make them reveal the supposedly concealed weapons. Four weeks ago they exiled fifteen men and their families, sending them to the desert city of [Rakka], three days journey south of here.

The Gendarmery Department seems to have full control of affairs and the Mutessarif upholds them. They are now holding about a hundred of the best citizens of the city in prison, and today the gendarmerie chief called the Armenian Bishop and told him that unless the Armenians deliver their arms and the revolutionists among them, that he has orders to exile the entire Armenian population of [Ourfa], as they did the people of [Zeitoun]. We know how the latter were treated, for hundreds of them have been dragged through [Ourfa] on their way to the desert whither they have been exiled. These poor exiles were mostly women, children and old men, and they were clubbed and beaten and lashed along as though they had been wild animals, and their women and girls were daily criminally outraged, both by their guards and the ruffians of every village, through which they passed, as the former allowed the latter to enter the camp of the exiles at night, and even distributed the girls among the villagers for the night. These poor victims of their oppressors' lust and hate might better have died by the bullet in their mountain home than be dragged about the country in this way. About two thousand of them have passed through [Ourfa] all more dead than alive; many hundreds have died from starvation and abuse along the roadside and nearly all are dying of starvation, thirst, of being kidnapped by the Anaza Arabs in the desert where they have been taken. We know how they are being treated because our exiles are in the same place, and one young Armenian doctor, who was there making medical examinations of soldiers for the government, has returned and told us.

XV

July 17, 1915. The refugees are "housed" principally in great camel stables and such like. It is a great camel region, the government having requisitioned 4,000 of these animals from there. The cattle and animals of the _____ were mostly requisitioned by the government en route. What they managed to conceal and bring with them has been put under requisition, but not taken. Meanwhile the owners are forbidden to sell, are unable to use, and are compelled to feed these animals, because the government holds them responsible to deliver them when called fro. I have before heard of refinements of devilry, but I have seen instances this year that have burned my soul. The manifest purpose to destroy these people by starvation cannot be denied.

XVI[*]

April 6, 1915. Every day 2,300 inhabitants from [Zeitoun] are transferred to [Marache] under severe guard, and after a short halt at night are deported toward unknown destinations. The hotels and the two Armenian schools are full of these deported families of [Zeitoun], [Alabache], and [Fernouz]. The government has decided to evacuate by force all the other Armenian regions. It is impossible to describe the misery which is resulting. Old men, invalids, children four or five years old go in masses barefooted.

April 27, 1915. Cruel perquisitions go on in all towns and villages of our province. All the higher class Armenians have been arrested and imprisoned at [Sivas]. The total number of these prisoners will soon reach 500 persons. They are taken as hostages without doubt. The situation is growing worse all the time, it threatens the very existence of the Armenian people.

May 27, 1915. Since the first days of April, caravans came from [Zeitoun] and environments going towards the south in the steppes of Mesopotamia. Talking only of those that crossed our city, the number of the deported rises to 6,700 persons. [Fernouz], [Kaban], [Alabache], and the whole region of [Zeitoun] have been evacuated. Bochnak mouhadjirs replace the Armenians thus exiled. The Turks are in a perfect delirium. It is impossible to describe the horrors suffered by the deported Armenians. Violation, conversion or rape of women and girls are ordinary and daily facts. The Armenian population of [Zeitoun] has been annihilated, one or two villages excepted. We are informed that 150 Armenians of [Hassan Beili] and 1,350 of [Deurtyol] have been deported to [Aleppo].

May 25, [1915]. The district of [Erzinghan], [Keghi], and [Baibourt] have been devastated by forced emigrations. The Armenian population of the city of [Erzeroum] has also received categoric orders to leave the city. They will be deported in mass; 160 merchants are already en route with their families. The government has confiscated their goods. We have no information about the deported people. They say they will be sent to [Mossoul].

The Young-Turk Government pursues unceasingly, and every day with added violence, the war to the finish that it has declared against its Armenian subjects. The provinces inhabited by Armenians, which were already under the reign of indescribable terror, have been evacuated by force. Thus the Armenian communities,

---

[*] Series of Reports from A.R.F. ("Dashnakzoutioun") of Sofia and statements by Miss Hunecke and Mr. Briquet communicated by Ambassador Morgenthau to Secretary of State, dated July 20 1915. National Archives (Washington DC), RG 59, 867.4016195. See *The Treatment of Armenians in the Ottoman Empire,* Report No 138. Latter includes passages dated April 6 and May 27 1915 (above) as letters from an Armenian inhabitant (name witheld) describing the deportation of Armenians from Cilicia; Report No 61 includes passage dated May 25 1915.

[at Samsoun, Trebizond, Sivas, Harpout, Amassia], and [Tokat, etc.], have been brutally deported, depraved of all their possessions, to the deserts of Mesopotamia. A great number of families have embraced Mohammedanism to escape a certain death.

June 18, 1915. (Extract from an official report.) The number of people from [Zeitoun] exiled to [Konia] is more than 6,000; they have been put in the Sandjak of [Soultanie] or [Karapounar]. More than 20,000 Armenians that have been forced to emigrate are thrown into the deserts amidst nomadic tribes, leaving their houses, gardens and tilled lands to the Turkish mouhajirs. Deprived of all that they possessed, the unfortunate people have not even any graves for their dead.

At [Aleppo] all the churches and schools are full of exiled Armenians. Rich and poor, teachers and pupils, all are brothers there, victims of the same blow. The inhabitants of the city do their utmost to alleviate the suffering. Those that are deported - women, old men, children - are obliged to cross the deserts on foot, under the burning sun, often deprived of food and water. The most modest complaint is stifled by the most barbarous threats. Overpowered by fatigue, exhausted by hunger, mothers in despair leave on the way their newborn children, often one-half year old, and continue their journey... Even in this deplorable state rapes and violent acts are everyday occurrences... The Armenians deported from [Hadjin] could not be recognized as a result of their trip of twelve days.

XVII[*]

FIRST EXODUS

The first group was not in a very bad state, because it was composed of the first families of the city, and they could in large part provide for their immediate needs (carriages and food). But a few days later, new bands appeared in most deplorable conditions; their number was nearly two thousand people.

Many, most of them went on foot, getting food every two or three days, and in general lacking the most necessary clothes. The Christian population of [Tarsous] tried to help them, but whatever their efforts, what they could do was like a drop of water in the ocean. Also they were not all allowed to enter the city; they had to sleep outdoors in no matter what weather, and the soldiers that kept them made all sorts of difficulties to the population of [Tarsous], which wanted to help the refugees. We saw some of them on the road. They went slowly, most of them fainting from want of food. We saw a father walking with a one-day-old baby in his arms, and behind him the mother walking as well as possible, pushed by the stick of the Turkish guardian. It was not uncommon to see a woman fall down and then rise again under

[*] *The Treatment of Armenians in the Ottoman Empire,* Report No 124, statement by Pierre Briquet (staff of St. Paul's Institute, Tarsus).

the stick. Some of them had a goat, a donkey, a mare. When they reached [Tarsous] they were obliged to sell them for five, ten, or fifteen piasters, because the Turkish soldiers took them away from them. I saw one who sold his goat to a Turk for six piasters. I saw an Armenian pushing two goats; a policeman (zabit) came, carried away the animals and, because the poor man protested, beat him mercilessly, until he fell in the dust senseless. Many Turks were present, no one stirred.

A young woman, whose husband had been imprisoned, was carried away with her fifteen-days-old baby, with a donkey for all luggage. After one day and a half of travel a soldier stole her donkey and she had to go on foot, her baby in her arms, from [Zeitoun] to [Aleppo].

A reporter, Mr [Schreiner], told us that while the refugees were going to [Bozanti], his carriage was stopped all the time by refugees asking for bread.

THIRD EXODUS

The third and last band counted 200 people. It reached [Tarsous] on May 13th, about seven o'clock. They were put in a Han, where I went to visit them. They had all come on foot from [Zeitoun] to [Tarsous], and had had nothing to eat for two days, days when it rained abundantly. Accompanied by one of my pupils, I made one or two translations from the Armenian, because we were under the surveillance of a policeman.

As soon as the Armenian refugees left their houses, mouhadjirs from Thrace (refugees) took possession of them. The former had been forbidden to take anything with them, and they themselves saw all their goods pass in other hands. There must be about 20,000 to 25,000 Turks in [Zeitoun] now, and the name of the town seems to have been changed into that of [Yeni Chehir (New City)].

I saw a girl three and a half years old, wearing only a shirt in rags. She had come on foot from [Zeitoun] to [Tarsous]. She was terribly spare and was shivering from cold, as were also all the innumerable children I saw on that day (Monday, May 14).

An Armenian told me that he had abandoned two children on the way because they could not walk, and that he did not know whether they had died of cold and hunger, whether a charitable soul had taken care of them, or whether they had become the prey of wild beasts. I learned later that this was far from being a unique case. Many children seem to have been thus abandoned. One seems to have been thrown in a well.

WHERE THE EXILES ARE

As I passed through [Konia], I went to see Dr. [Dodd], and this is what he told me: When the first refugees from [Zeitoun] came to [Konia], the Christian population bought food and clothes for them; but the Vali refused to allow them any communication with the refugees, pretending that they had all that they wanted. A few days later, however, they could get the help they needed. The fact is that the government gave them only very bad bread every two or three days. Dr. [Dodd] told me that a woman threw her dying baby from the window of the train.

The refugees of [Zeitoun] have been directed to [Kara-Pounar], one of the most unhealthy places of the vilayet of [Konia], situated between [Konia] and [Eregli], but nearer the latter. Many of them died and the mortality is increasing every day. The malaria makes ravages among them, because of the complete lack of food and shelter. How cruelly ironic to think that the government pretends to be sending them there to found a colony; and they have no ploughs, no seeds to sow, no bread, no abode; in fact, they are sent with empty hands.

One part only seems to be at [Kara-Pounar]; the other inhabitants from [Zeitoun] seem to have been sent to [Deir-el-Zor], on the Euphrates; their condition is still worse and they ask as a favor to be sent to [Kara-Pounar].

In [Tarsous]. A great panic reigns among the Armenian population in _____ because it was said that they were also to be exiled. But nothing has happened yet.

In [Konia]. More than 200 Armenians have been sent to [Kara-Pounarl. Among them is Mr [Haigazian], president of the College of [Konia]. On Thursday 90 people were notified to be ready to leave on Saturday, May 26. The Armenians dare not leave their houses.

XVIII[*]

TESTIMONY OF WIDOW [VICTORIA KHATCHADOUR BARUTJIBASHIAN] OF [BAIBOURT].

A week before anything was done to [Baibourt], the villages all around had been emptied and their inhabitants had become victims of the gendarmes and marauding bands. Three days before the starting of the Armenians from after a week's imprisonment, Bishop [(Dzairakouin Vartabed) Der Anania Hazarabedian] has been hanged, with seven other notables. After these hangings, seven or eight other notables were killed in their own houses for refusing to go out of the city. Seventy or eighty other Armenians, after being beaten in prison, were taken to the woods and killed. The Armenian population of [Baibourt] was sent off in three batches; I was among the third batch. My husband died eight years ago, leaving me and my eight-year-old daughter and my mother extensive possessions, so that we were living in comfort. Since mobilization began, the Commandant has been living in my house

---

[*] Testimony-report (n/d) forwarded by Ambassador Morgenthau to Secretary of State, dated August 10 1915. National Archives (Washington DC), RG 59, 867.4016/122. See *The Treatment of Armenians in the Ottoman Empire*, No 59.

free of rent. He told me not to go, but I felt I must share the fate of my people. I took three horses with me, loaded with provisions. My daughter had some five-lira pieces around her neck, and I carried some twenty liras and four diamond rings on my person. All else that we had was left behind. Our party left June 1 (old style), fifteen gendarmes going with us. The party numbered four or five hundred persons. We had got only two hours away from home when bands of villagers and brigands in large numbers, with rifles, guns, axes, etc., surrounded us on the road, and robbed us of all we had. The gendarmes took my three horses and sold them to Turkish mouhadjirs, pocketing the money. They took my money and that from my daughter's neck, also all our food. After this they separated the men, one by one, and shot them all within six or seven days — every male above 15 years old. By my side were killed two priests, one of them over 90 years of age. These bandsmen took all the good-looking women and carried them off on their horses. Very many women and girls were thus carried off to the mountains, among them my sister, whose one-year-old baby they threw away; a Turk picked it up and carried it off, I know not where. My mother walked till she could walk no farther, and dropped by the roadside on a mountain-top. We found on the road many of those who had been in the previous sections carried from [Baibourt]; some women were among the killed, with their husbands and sons. We also came across some old people and little infants still alive but in a pitiful condition, having shouted their voices away. We were not allowed to sleep at night in the villages, but lay down outside. Under cover of the night indescribable deeds were committed by the gendarmes, bandsmen and villagers. Many of us died from hunger and strokes of apoplexy. Others were left by the roadside, too feeble to go on.

One morning we saw fifty to sixty wagons with about thirty Turkish widows, whose husbands had been killed in the war: and these were going to Constantinople. One of these women made a sign to one of the gendarmes to kill a certain Armenian whom she pointed out. The gendarmes asked her if she did not wish to kill him herself, at which she said "Why not?" and, drawing a revolver from her pocket, shot and killed him. Each one of these Turkish hanums had five or six Armenian girls of ten or under with her. Boys the Turks never wished to take: they killed all, of whatever age. These women wanted to take my daughter, too, but she would not be separated from me. Finally we were both taken into their wagons on our promising to become Moslem. As soon as we entered the araba, they began to teach us how to be Moslems, and changed our names, calling me [Nadjie] and her [Nourié].

The worst and most unimaginable horrors were reserved for us at the banks of the Euphrates and in the Erzingian plain. The mutilated bodies of women, girls and little children made everybody shudder The bandsmen were doing all sorts of awful deeds to the women and girls that were with us, whose cries went up to heaven. At the Euphrates, the bandsmen and gendarmes threw into the river all the remaining children under fifteen years old. Those that could swim were shot down as they struggled in the water.

After seven days we reached [Ezingian]. Not an Armenian was left alive there. The Turkish women took my daughter and me to the bath, and there showed us many other women and girls that had accepted Islam. Between there and [Enderes], the fields and hillsides were dotted with swollen and blackened corpses that filled and fouled the air with their stench. On this road we met six women wearing the feradje and with children in their arms. But when the gendarmes lifted their veils, they found that they were men in disguise, so they shot them. After thirty-two days' journey we reached [Constantinople].

XIX

THE HORRORS OF _____

The forced exodus from_____of the last part of the population took place on June 1, 1914. All the villages, as well as three-quarters of the town, had already been evacuated. An escort of fifteen gendarmes followed the third convoy, which included 4,000 to 5,000 persons. The prefect of the city had wished them a pleasant journey. But at a few hours' distance from the town, the caravan was surrounded by bands of the _____ and by a mob of Turkish peasants armed with guns, axes and clubs. They first began plundering the deported, searching carefully even the very young children. The gendarmes sold to the Turkish peasants what they could not carry away with them. After having taken even the food of those unhappy people, the massacre of the males began, including two priests, one of whom was ninety. In six or seven days all men below 15 had been murdered. It was the beginning of the end. People on horseback raised the veils of the women, and carried off the pretty ones.

On the way we constantly met murdered men and youths, all covered with blood. There were also women and girls killed near their husbands or sons. On the heights of the mountains and in the depths of the valleys numbers of old men and babies were lying on the ground. During the night the caravan was not allowed to stop in the villages; they all had to sleep on the ground, exposed to the unwarrantable barbarism of the Turkish bands and peasants. The poor people found themselves in the necessity of eating grass. Sometimes the gendarmes distributed among them a small piece of hard bread. Many hungry people died of all that suffering.

_____, June 25 (old style). (From a private letter):

The Armenian population has been converted to Islamism; it was a means of escaping from the forced migration. Orthodox Turks are given the wives of absent husbands or their daughters. We have been told that according to an order from the Padishah, everybody must embrace Islamism.

At Cesarea, Sivas, Trebizond, Ordoo, and many other towns and cities, thousands have been persuaded by threats and by abominable tortures to embrace the Mohammedan faith. In many cases the wives and daughters of Christians have been immediately compelled to marry Turks.

All over the country leading Armenians have been shot or hanged. Leading merchants have been beggared and exiled. Thirty thousand Mohammedan criminals have been released from jail and formed into bands under strict military discipline. One of the duties of these bands is to pillage villages and to rob and assassinate exiles.

The Greek and Armenian Patriarchs have been refused audiences with the ministers of the Turkish Government. Foreign Ambassadors, among them the United States Ambassador, have been rebuffed and told that what the Imperial Government wishes to do with its subjects is none of their business.

Turkish ministers and other officials have repeatedly avowed the intention to smash the Christian nationalities and thus forever put an end to the Armenian question.

XXI[*]

July 13. After we had seen thousands of people start out, and especially after ours had actually gone, we came to the conclusion that if anything could be done to stop this terrible crime, which impresses us as ten times worse than any massacre, it would be done in Constantinople. In Constantinople we found that the whole plan of deportation is one of the central government and that no pressure from the embassies had been able to do anything.

We believe there is imminent danger of many of these people, whom we estimate for the Sivas, Erzroom and Harpoot vilayets, to be 600,000 starving to death on the road. They took food a few days, but did not dare take much money with them, for, if they did so, it is doubtful whether they would be allowed to keep it.

We met on the road near _____ people of two villages of which the people were going on foot with less than a donkey to a family, no food, nor bedding, hardly any men, and many of the women barefooted and carrying children. A case in _____ worthy of notice was that of F's sister. Her husband had worked in our hospital as a soldier-nurse for many months. She contracted typhus and was brought to our hospital. Her mother, a woman of 60 to 70, got up from a sick bed to go out and care for their seven children, the oldest of which was about 12. A few days before the deportation, the husband was imprisoned and exiled without examination or fault. When the quarter in which they lived went, the mother got out of bed in the hospital, and was put on an ox-cart to go with her children.

---

[*] Letter dated 13th July 1915, from the Rev. Ernest C. Partridge. *The Treatment of Armenians in the Ottoman Empire*, Report No 77.

XXII[*]

August 3. The idea of direct attack and massacre that was carried out in former times has been altered somewhat, in that the men and boys have been deported from their homes in great numbers and disappeared en route, and later on the women and children have been made to follow. For some time stories have been prevalent from travelers arriving from the interior of the killing of the males, of great numbers of bodies along the road-sides, and floating in the Euphrates river; of the delivery to the Kurds by the gendarmes accompanying the convoys of women and children of all the younger members of the parties; of unthinkable outrages committed by gendarmes and Kurds, and even the killing of many of the victims. At first these stories were not given much credence, but as many of the refugees are now arriving in [Aleppo], no doubt longer remains of the truth of the matter. August 2nd about 800 middle-aged and old women, and children under the age of 10 years, arrived afoot from Diarbekir after 45 days en route, and in the most pitiable condition imaginable. They report the taking of all the young women and girls by the Kurds, the pillaging even of the last bit of money and other belongings, of starvation, of privation, and hardship of every description. Their deplorable condition bears out their statements in every detail.

I am informed that 4,500 persons were sent from Sughurt to Ras-el-Ain, over 2,000 from Mezireh to Diarbekir, and that all the cities of Bitlis, Mardin, Mossoul, Severek, Malatia, Besne, etc., have been depopulated of Armenians, the men and boys and many of the women killed, and the balance scattered throughout the country. If this is true, of which there is little doubt, even the latter must naturally die of fatigue, hunger and disease. The Governor of Deir-el-Zor on the Euphrates river, and who is now in _____, says there are 15,000 Armenian refugees in that city. Children are frequently sold to prevent starvation, as the government furnishes practically no subsistence. The following statistics show the number of families and persons arriving in places from whence deported, and number sent further on, up to and including July 30:

---

[*] Consular report from Aleppo, J.B. Jackson to Secretary of State, dated August 3 1915. National Archives (Washington DC), RG 59, 867.4016/129. See *The Treatment of Armenians in the Ottoman Empire*, Report No 139 (b), from series of reports from Mr. Jackson, U.S. Consul at Aleppo.

WHERE, FROM	FAMILIES	PERSONS	SENT AWAY
Cheuk-Merzemen (Dortyol)	400	2,109	734
Ojakli	115	537	137
Euzerli	116	593	173
Hasanbayli	187	1,118	514
Harni	84	528	34
Karspazar	51	340	
Hadjin	592	3,988	1,025
Roumlou	51	388	296
Shar	150	1,112	357
Sis	231	1,317	
Bagche	13	68	
Dengala	126	804	
Drtadli	12	104	
Zeytoun	5	8	
Tarpouz	22	97	
Albustan	10	44	
Total	2,165	13,255	3,270

2,100 persons more arrived since the above figures were compiled.

Now all Armenians have been ordered deported from the cities of Aintab, Mardin, Bitlis, Antioch, Alexandretta, Kessab, and all the smaller towns in Aleppo province, estimated at 60,000 persons. It is natural to suppose that they will suffer the fate of those that have gone before, and which is appalling to contemplate. The results are that as 90 per cent of the commerce of the interior is in the hands of the Armenians, the country is facing ruin. The great bulk of business being done on credit, hundreds of prominent business men other than Armenians face bankruptcy. There will not be left in the places evacuated a single tanner, moulder, blacksmith, tailor, carpenter, clay worker, weaver, shoemaker, jeweler, pharmacist, doctor, lawyer, or any of the professional or tradesmen, with very few exceptions, and the country will be left in a practically helpless state.

The important American religious and educational institutions in this region are losing their professors, teachers, helpers, and students, and even the orphanages are to be emptied of the hundreds of children therein, which ruins the fruits of 50 years of untiring effort in this field. The government officials in a mocking way ask what the Americans are going to do with these establishments now that the Armenians are being done away with.

The situation is becoming more critical daily, as there is no telling where this thing will end. The Germans are being blamed on every hand, for if they have not directly ordered this wholesale slaughter (for it is nothing less than the extermination of the Armenian race) they at least condone it.

XXIII[*]

July 12. In Der-el-Zor, a great city in the wilderness, six day's journey from Aleppo, we found a large Khan overflowing. Every available space, even roofs and porches, were occupied by the Armenians. Mostly women and children, as well as a number of men, had spread something over their heads, in order to keep themselves in the shade.

As soon as I heard that they were Armenians, I went to them to talk with them. They were the people of Furnus, from the region of Zeitoun and Marash, who had been huddled together in this narrow place, and had an extremely sorrowful look on their faces. After an inquiry, I found out that one of Miss Rhoner's pupils, Martha Karabashian, from the orphanage of Marash, was among the crowd. She related to me the following: The Turkish Zaptiehs came to Furnus one day and took a great number of men by force and carried them away to become soldiers. Where they were to be used was not made known, neither to them nor to their families. Then they told those that were left behind that they had to desert their houses within four hours. They allowed them to carry as much of their possessions as they could carry with themselves, also their horses. At the expiration of the appointed time the poor people were taken out of their village, under the guidance of the soldiers, not knowing whither they were going, or whether they would see it again. At first, so long as they were in their own mountains, and had something to eat, everything went all right. They had promised to give them money and bread, and at first they gave daily 30 paras (3 cents) per head. But very soon the promised ration was withheld, and they gave us only 30 dramms of bulghur every day per head. In this way the people of Furnus arrived at Der-el-Zor, after four weeks of exhausting journey, through Marash and Aleppo. They had been in the inn three weeks, and knew not what would come to them next. They had no money, and the food given by the Turks had become very sparing. For many days they had not had any bread. In cities the soldiers had shut them up at nights, and had not allowed them to talk with the residents. So, Martha had not been permitted to go to the orphanage in Marash. She told to me very sadly: "We had two houses and we had to leave everything; now muhadjirs occupy our houses." There had been no massacre in Furnus, and they had been favored with bread and water during their march through the scorching wilderness.

The Armenians themselves did not know the reason of their expulsion.

---

[*] Letter dated 12 July 1915, from Schwester L. Möhring, a German missionary, describing her journey from Baghdad to the passes of Amanus, published in the German journal *Sonnenaufgang,* September 1915. *The Treatment of Armenians in the Ottoman Empire,* Report No 145.

The next day, about the time of noon-rest, we met a large group of Armenians. The poor people had built protections of goats' hair, according to the primitive Kurdish ways, and were resting under them. But the greater part of the people were without a shelter, sitting on the burning sand, under the scorching sun. On account of many sick ones, the Turks allowed them a day of rest. One can never imagine such a comfortless group of people in the wilderness, under such unbearable circumstances. From the clothes they gave the appearance of belonging to the wealthy class. Some had been sent to the province of Konia, and a large number to the various villages of Zor beyond Aleppo, and to the surrounding districts of Aleppo—-Munbej, Bab, Maara, Idlib, etc. The deportation is still going on. Adana, Mersin, Hadjin, Sis and other places will no doubt undergo the same fate, according to news received by us.

All these people are being removed without any of their goods and chattels, and to such places where the climate is totally unsuited to them. They are left without shelter, without food, and without clothing, depending only upon the morsels of bread which the government will throw before them, a government which is unable even to feed its own troops. It is impossible to read or to hear, without shedding tears, even the meager details of these deportations. There are only 50 males among the thousand families exiled to Soultanieh. Most of the families have traveled on foot, old men and children have died on the way, young women in childbirth have been left on mountain passes, and at least 10 deaths a day are recorded among them, even in their place of exile - victims of hunger and sickness.

XXIV[*]

If it were simply a matter of being obliged to leave here to go somewhere else, it would not be so bad, but everybody knows it is a case of going to one's death. If there was any doubt about it, it has been removed by the arrival of a number of parties, aggregating several thousand people, from Erzroom and Erzinggan. I have visited their encampment a number of times and talked with some of the people. A more pitiable sight cannot be imagined. They are, almost without exception, ragged, filthy, hungry and sick. That is not surprising, in view of the fact that they have been on the road for nearly two months, with no change of clothing, no chance to wash, no shelter, and little to eat. The government has been giving them some scanty rations here. I watched them one time when their food was brought. Wild animals could not be worse. They rushed upon the guards who carried the food and the guards beat them back with clubs, hitting hard enough to kill them sometimes. To watch them one could hardly believe that these people were human beings.

[*] Consular report from Harput, Leslie A. Davis to Secretary of State, dated August 10 1915, National Archives (Washington DC), RG 59, 867.4016/122. See *The Treatment of Armenians in the Ottoman Empire,* Report No 65.

As one walks through the camp, mothers offer their children and beg one to take them. In fact, the Turks have been taking their choice of these children and girls for slaves, or worse. In fact, they have even had their doctors there to examine the more likely girls and thus secure the best ones.

There are very few men among them, as most of them have been killed on the road. All tell the same story of having been attacked and robbed by the Kurds. Most of them were attacked over and over again, and a great many of them, especially the men, were killed. Women and children were also killed. Many died, of course, from sickness and exhaustion on the way, and there have been deaths each day that they have been here. Several different parties have arrived and, after remaining a day or two, have been pushed on with no apparent destination. Those who have reached here are only a small portion, however, of those who started. By continuing to drive these people on in this way it will be possible to dispose of all of them in a comparatively short time. Among those with whom I have talked were three sisters. They had been educated at [Constantinople] and spoke excellent English. They said their family was the richest in [Erzeroum] and numbered twenty-five when they left, but there were now only fourteen survivors. The other eleven, including the husband of one of them and their old grandmother, had been butchered before their eyes by the Kurds. The oldest male survivor of the family was eight years of age. When they left [Erzeroum] they had money, horses and personal effects, but they had been robbed of everything, including even their clothing. They said some of them had been left absolutely naked and others with only a single garment. When they reached a village their gendarmes obtained clothes for them from some of the native women. Another girl with whom I talked is the daughter of the Protestant pastor of [Erzeroum]. She said every member of her family with her had been killed and she was left entirely alone. These and some others are a few survivors of the better class of people who have been exiled. They are being detained in an abandoned schoolhouse just outside of the town, and no one is allowed to enter it. They said they practically were in prison, although they were allowed to visit a spring just outside the building. It was there I happened to see them. All the others are camped in a large open field with no protection at all from the sun.

The condition of these people indicates clearly the fate of those who have left and are about to leave from here. I believe nothing has been heard from any of them as yet, and probably very little will be heard. The system that is being followed seems to be to have bands of Kurds awaiting them on the road to kill the men especially and incidentally some of the others. The entire movement seems to be the most thoroughly organized and effective massacre this country has ever seen.

Not many men have been spared, however, to accompany those who are being sent into exile, for a more prompt and sure method has been used to dispose of them. Several thousand Armenian men have been arrested during the past few weeks. These have been put in prison, and each time that several hundred had been gathered up in that way they were sent away during the night. The first lot were sent away during the night of June 23rd. Among them were some of the professors in the American College and other prominent Armenians, including the Prelate of the Armenian Gregorian Church. There have been frequent rumors that all of these were killed, and there is little doubt that they were. All Armenian soldiers have likewise been sent away in the same manner. They have been arrested and confined in a building at one end of the town. No distinction has been made between those who had paid their military exemption tax and those who had not. Their money was accepted and then they were arrested and sent off with the others. It was said that they were to go somewhere to work on the roads but no one had heard from them, and that is undoubtedly false.

The fate of all the others has been pretty well established by reliable reports of a similar occurrence on Wednesday, July 7th. On Monday many men were arrested, both at [Harpout] and [Mezreh] and put in prison. At daybreak Tuesday morning they were taken out and made to march towards an almost uninhabited mountain. There were about eight hundred in all, and they were tied together in groups of fourteen each. That afternoon they arrived in a small Kurdish village, where they were kept overnight in the mosque and other buildings. During all this time they were without food or water. All their money and much of their clothing had been taken from them. On Wednesday morning they were taken to a valley a few hours distant, where they were all made to sit down. Then the gendarmes began shooting them, until they had killed nearly all of them. Some who had not been killed by bullets were then disposed of with knives and bayonets. A few succeeded in breaking the rope with which they were tied to their companions and running away, but most of these were pursued and killed. A few succeeded in getting away, probably not more than two or three. Among those who were killed was the treasurer of the American College. Many other estimable men were among the number. No charge of any kind had ever been made against any of these men. They were simply arrested and killed as part of the general plan to dispose of the Armenian race.

Last night several hundred more men, including both men arrested by the civil authorities and those enrolled as soldiers, were taken in a different direction and murdered in a similar manner. It is said this happened at a place not two hours distant from here. I shall ride out that way some day when things become a little quieter and try to verify it for myself.

The same thing has been done systematically in the villages. A few weeks ago about three hundred men were gathered together at Itchma and Haboosi, two villages four and five hours distant from here, and then taken up into the mountains and massacred. This seems to be fully established. Many women from those villages have been here since and told about it. There have been rumors of similar occurrences in other places.

There seems to be a definite plan to dispose of all the Armenian men, but after the departure of the families during the first few days of the enforcement of the order it was announced that the women and children with no men in the family might remain here for the present, and many hoped the worst was over. The American missionaries began considering plans to aid the women and children who would be left here with no means of support. It was thought that perhaps an orphanage could be opened to care for some of the children, and especially those who had been born in America and then brought here by their parents, and also those who belonged to parents who had been connected in some way with the American mission and schools. There would be plenty of opportunity, although there might not be sufficient means, to care for children who reached here with the exiles from other vilayets and whose parents had died on the way. I went to see the Vali about this matter yesterday and was met with a flat refusal. He said we could aid these people if we wished to do so, but the government was establishing orphanages for the children and we could not undertake any work of that nature. An hour after I left the Vali the announcement was made that all the Armenians remaining here, including women and children, must leave on July 13.

XXV[*]

The first of August the beating began in the church. The object of this was to force the people to bring any ammunition and firearms they might have. Most of the people accepted their fate in silence. A mother threw herself in front of her consumptive son and herself received the stripes. A German woman tried to save her Armenian husband. "Get out of the way or I will beat you" cried the official.

"I don't care for the emperor himself; my orders come from Talat Bey."

Some Armenian ladies came to intercede with the official, and for a day or two the beatings were less vigorous.

Then came the awful Saturday, the day of darkness and horror. Women came to our house saying, "They are beating the Armenian men to death and they are going to beat the women next!" I ran to a neighbor's house and there found men and women crying. The men had gotten out of the church and were telling their story. "They are

[*] Statement dated September 24 1915 by Miss Holt, of the American Mission Station at Ada-Pazar. *The Treatment of Armenians in the Ottoman Empire,* Report No 102.

beating the men frightfully," they cried. "They say they will throw us into the river; they will send us into exile; they will make Mohammedans of us; they will beat our women next; they are coming to the house."

There was one Turkish soldier outside of the church in tears. He said he had been crying three days and nights because of the awful treatment of the Armenian people. Some of the people were shut up ten days in the church.

Three days after the beating ceased, and we were beginning to take courage again; a few Armenian shops were opened; but the next morning early, which was Sunday, news came that all the Armenians in [Adapazar], numbering about 25,000, were to be sent into exile. They were to go to Konia by freight train, if they could pay their passage, and then to Mosul by carriage - on foot a journey of weeks and months. Such awful stories came to us about things that had happened to those who went by foot that people sold their last possessions to get enough to pay their train passage. They were afraid to take money with them. The poor had none to take. The rich must leave all their property behind. If they took money they feared violence. By Wednesday there was no freight trains to send them by, as so many had gone, but all the people were turned out in the streets to await their turn—many for several days.

* * *

In response to the urgent appeal of Ambassador Morgenthau the Committee on Armenian Atrocities, in co-operation with the Committee of Mercy, has decided to make a wide appeal for funds. Several gentlemen have already pledged large contributions, but the need is very great, and it is expected that a good number of smaller gifts will be received.

The crimes now being perpetrated upon the Armenian people surpass in their horror and cruelty anything that history has recorded during the past thousand years. The educated and the ignorant, the rich and the poor, are all being subjected to every form of barbarity and outrage.

It is understood, however, that very many Turks are opposed to this policy of persecution. It is hoped that prompt action will make it possible to save a great many lives, and repatriate some at least of those who have been driven from their homes.

Funds will be forwarded to the Ambassador as fast as received. Donations should be sent to the Treasurer, Mr Charles R. Crane, 70 Fifth Avenue, New York City, N.Y.

Circulated to the King and War Cabinet.

ARMENIAN MASSACRES.

Report by an eye-witness, Lieut. Sayied Ahmed Moukhtar Baas

In April 1915 I was quartered at Erzeroum. An order came from Constantinople that Armenians inhabiting the frontier towns and villages be deported to the interior. It was said then that this was only a precautionary measure. I saw at that time large convoys of Armenians go through Erzeroum. They were mostly old men, women and children. Some of the able-bodied men had fled to Russia. The massacres had not begun yet. In May 1915 I was transferred to Trebizond. In July an order came to deport to the interior all the Armenians in the Vilayet of Trebizond. Being a member of the Court martial I knew that deportations meant massacres.

The Armenian Bishop of Trebizond was ordered to proceed under escort to Erzeroum to answer for charges trumped up against him. But instead of Erzeroum he was taken to Baipurt and from there to Gumush-Khana. The Governor of the latter place was then Colonel Abdul-Kader Aintabli of the General Staff. He is famous for his atrocities against Armenians. He had the Bishop murdered at night. The Bishop of Erzeroum was also murdered at Gumush-Khana.

Besides the deportation order referred to above, an imperial "Iradeh" was issued ordering that all deserters, when caught, should be shot without trial. The secret order read "Armenians" in lieu of "deserters." The Sultan's "Iradeh" was accompanied by a "fetwa" from Sheikh-ul-Islam stating that the Armenians had shed Moslem blood and their killing was lawful. Then the deportations started. The children were kept back at first. The Government opened up a school for the grown up children and the American Consul of Trebizond instituted an asylum for the infants. When the first batches of the deported Armenians arrived at Gumush-Khana all able-bodied men were sorted out with the excuse that they were going to be given work. The women and children were sent ahead under escort with the assurance by the Turkish authorities that their final destination was Mosul and that no harm will befall them. The men kept behind were taken out of town in batches of 15 or 20, lined up on the edge of ditches prepared beforehand, shot and thrown into the ditches. Hundreds of men were shot every day in a similar manner. The women and children were attacked on their way by the ("Shotas") the armed bands organised by the Turkish Government who attacked them and seized a certain number. After

---

[*] The minutes accompanying these two reports attest to their authenticity. Both were forwarded to the Foreign Office by Sir Mark Sykes in 1916. See PRO, FO 371/2768/261608, 261609.

plundering and committing the most dastardly outrages on the women and children they massacred them in cold blood. These attacks were a daily occurrence until every woman and child had been got rid of. The military escorts had strict orders not to interfere with the "Shotas".

The children that the Government had taken in charge were also deported and massacred.

The infants in the care of the American Consul at Trebizond were taken away with the pretext that they were going to be sent to Sivas where an asylum had been prepared for them. They were taken out to sea in little boats. At some distance out they were stabbed to death, put in sacks and thrown into the sea. A few days later some of their little bodies were washed up on the shore at Trebizond.

In July 1915 I was ordered to accompany a convoy of deported Armenians. It was the last batch from Trebizond. There were in the convoy 120 men, 700 children and about 400 women. From Trebizond I took them to Gumish-Khana. Here the 120 men were taken away, and, as I was informed later, they were all killed. At Gumish-Khana I was ordered to take the women and children to Ezinjian. On the way I saw thousands of bodies of Armenians unburied. Several bands of "Shotas" met us on the way and wanted me to hand over to them women and children. But I persistently refused. I did leave on the way about 200 children with Moslem families who were willing to take care of them and educate them. The "Mutessarrif" of Erzinjian ordered me to proceed with the convoy to Kamack. At the later place the authorities refused to take charge of the women and children. I fell ill and wanted to go back, but I was told that as long as the Armenians in my charge were alive I would be sent from one place to the other. However I managed to include my batch with the deported Armenians that had come from Erzeroum. In charge of the later was a colleague of mine Mohamed Effendi from the Gendarmerie. He told me afterwards that after leaving Kamach they came to a valley where the Euphrates ran. A band of Shotas sprang out and stopped the convoy. They ordered the escort to keep away and then shot every one of the Armenians and threw them in the river.

At Trebizond the Moslems were warned that if they sheltered Armenians they would be liable to the death penalty.

Government officials at Trebizond picked up some of the prettiest Armenian women of the best families. After committing the worst outrages on them they had them killed.

Cases of rape of women and girls even publicly are very numerous. They were systematically murdered after the outrage.

The Armenians deported from Erzeroum started with their cattle and whatever possessions they could carry. When they reached Erzinjian they became suspicious seeing that all the Armenians had already been deported. The Vali of Erzeroum allayed their fears and assured them most solemnly that no harm would befall them. He told them that the first convoy should leave for Kamach, the others remaining at Erzeroum until they received word from their friends informing of their safe arrival to destination. And so it happened. Word came that the first batch had arrived safely at Kamach, which was true enough. But the men were kept at Kamach and shot, and the women and children were massacred by the Shotas after leaving that town.

The Turkish officials in charge of the deportation and extermination of the Armenians were: At Erzeroum, Bihaa Eddin Shaker Bey; At Trebizond; Naiil Bey, Tewfik Bey Monastirly, Colonel of Gendarmerie, The Commissioner of Police; At Kemach; The member of Parliament for Erzinjian. The Shotas headquarters were also known. Their chief was the Kurd Murzabey who boasted that he alone had killed 70,000 Armenians. Afterwards he was thought to be dangerous by the Turks and thrown into prison charged with having hit a gendarme. He was eventually executed in secret.

* * *

Circulated to The King and War Cabinet

ARMENIAN MASSACRES

Report by an eye-witness. Lt. Hassan Maaroue

In August 1915 in the suburbs of Mush I saw large numbers of dead bodies of Armenians, men, women and children lying in the fields. Some had been shot, some stabbed and most of them had been horribly mutilated. The women were mostly naked.

In the villages around Mush I saw old women and children wandering in the streets, haggard and emaciated.

In the same month, in a camp outside Bitlis I saw collected about 500 women, girls and children guarded by gendarmes. I asked the latter what was to become of these people. They said that they were being deported but that they had orders to let the Bands deal with them on the way. The Bands had been organised by the Turkish Government for the purpose of massacring the Armenians. They were formed by Kurds, Turkish gendarmes and criminals who had been specially set free.

On the river at Bitlis I saw quite a number of bodies of Armenians floating on the water, and some washed up on the banks. The smell was pestilential and the water undrinkable.

In the same month of August in the country at a distance of about two hours from Zaart, I saw the bodies of about 15,000 massacred Armenians. They were piled up on top of each other in two ravines. The Armenian Bishop of Zaart was, at his own request, taken to a cave near by and shot.

On my return from Zaart to Mush in a village of the suburbs of Mush over 500 Armenians mostly women and children were herded up in a stable and locked in. The gendarmes threw flaming torches through an opening in the ceiling. They were all burnt alive. I did not go near, but I distinctly saw the flames and heard the screams of the poor victims.

I heard from reliable persons that women in the family way had their bodies cut open and the child snatched out and thrown away.

At Mush the streets were strewn with bodies of Armenians. Every time an Armenian ventured out of doors, [he] was instantly killed.

Even men of great age, blind and invalids were not spared.

From Mush to Hinis at short distances from each other I saw piles of bodies of Armenians in the fields alongside the road.

Between Sherkes-Koi and Hinis I saw two ravines filled with corpses of Armenians about 400 in each ravine mostly men. Another ravine was filled with bodies of little children.

At Khara-Shuban I saw a large number of bodies of Armenians floating on the river Murad.

When I went to Erzinjian I was told that wholesale massacres were perpetrated at Erzinjian, Mamakhatoun and the whole country round. Besides those that the Turks had killed and burnt alive they threw thousands of them in the Euphrates. A large number of Armenians seeing that their death was inevitable, and fearing worse atrocities, preferred to throw themselves in the Euphrates.

ԿԻ

Gomidas Institute
Armenian Genocide Documentation Series

Maria Jacobsen (Kristen Vind, transl., Ara Sarafian ed. and intro.), *Diaries of a Danish Missionary: Harpoot, 1907-1919.*

Tacy Atkinson (J. Michael Hagopian ed. and intro.), *"The German, the Turk and the Devil Made a Triple Alliance": Harpoot Diaries, 1908-1917.*

Henry Riggs (Ara Sarafian, ed.), *Days of Tragedy in Armenia: Personal Experiences in Harpoot, 1915-1917.*

James Barton (Ara Sarafian, ed. and intro.), *"Turkish Atrocities": Statements of American Missionaries on the Destruction of Christian Communities in Ottoman Turkey, 1915-1917,*

Bertha Morley (Hilmar Kaiser, ed.), *Marsovan 1915: The Diaries of Bertha Morley.*

Eberhard Count Wolffskeel Von Reichenberg, (Hilmar Kaiser ed. and intro.), *Zeitoun, Mousa Dagh, Ourfa: Letters on the Armenian Genocide.*

James Bryce and Arnold Toynbee (Ara Sarafian, ed. and intro), *Treatment of Armenians in the Ottoman Empire, 1915-1916: Documents Presented to Viscount Grey of Fallodon by Viscount Bryce: Uncensored Edition.*

FURTHER READINGS FROM STERNDALE CLASSICS

Ottoman Empire and WWI
Lewis Einstein, *The Dardanelles Campaign.*
George Hornton, *The Blight of Asia.*
Grace Knapp, *The Tragedy of Bitlis.*
Henry Morgenthau, *Ambassador Morgenthau's Story.*
Rafael de Nogales, *Four Years Beneath the Crescent.*
Harry Stuermer, *Inside Constantinople.*
Clarence Ussher, *An American Physician in Turkey.*

Ottoman Empire and Provinces
Childs, *Across Asia Minor on Foot.*
Curzon, *Armenia: A Year in Erzeroom.*
George Hamilton, *Through Armenia on Horseback.*
William Ramsay, *Impressions of Turkey.*

Ottoman Empire and the Eastern Question
Duke of Argyll, *Our Responsibilities for Turkey.*